W9-BAJ-728

CULTURE SMART!

# SWITZERLAND

Kendall Maycock

Graphic Arts Center Publishing®

First published in Great Britain 2004
by Kuperard, an imprint of Bravo Ltd.

Series Editor  Geoffrey Chesler
Design  DW Design

Simultaneously published in the U.S.A. and Canada
by Graphic Arts Center Publishing Company
P. O. Box 10306, Portland, OR 97296-0306


Library of Congress Cataloging-in-Publication Data

Maycock, Kendall.
Switzerland : a quick guide to customs and etiquette / Kendall Maycock.
p. cm. – (Culture smart!)
Includes bibliographical references and index.
ISBN 1-55868-799-8 (softbound)
1. Switzerland–Social life and customs–20th century. 2. Switzerland–
Description and travel. 3. Etiquette–Switzerland. 4. National
characteristics, Swiss. I. Title. II. Series.

DQ36.M373 2004
914.9404'74--dc22

                           2004004106


Printed in Hong Kong

Cover image: Ski resort, Kandersteg.
*Travel Ink/Jill Swainson*

**CultureShock!**Consulting and **Culture Smart!** guides both contribute
to and regularly feature in the weekly travel program "Fast Track" on
BBC World TV.

## About the Author

KENDALL MAYCOCK is a Canadian author and journalist living in Zurich. After graduating in political science from the University of Calgary she worked for an independent newspaper in South Africa, where she met her Swiss husband. Her book *Black Taxi: Shooting South Africa* documents her experiences there. She has contributed cultural essays to the *Washington Times* magazine "The World and I," and writes a monthly column for the Swiss parenting magazine *The New Stork Times* about life as an expatriate resident coming to terms with, and growing to love, her adopted Switzerland.

## Other Books in the Series

Other titles are in preparation. For more information, contact: info@kuperard.co.uk

The publishers would like to thank **CultureShock!**Consulting for its help in researching and developing the concept for this series.

# contents

# contents

# Map of Switzerland

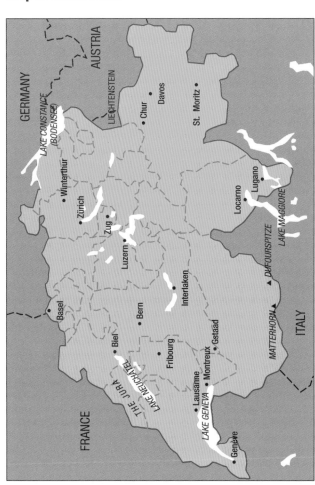

# introduction

Set aside your preconceptions of postcard scenery, chocolate and cheese, faceless bankers, and spotless cities. The real Switzerland is anything but bland. This small, rugged, landlocked country at the heart of Europe is full of surprises. Largely victims of their own success, the Swiss have often been misunderstood. Having escaped the traumas of war in the last century, they did not have to rebuild a shattered society. Their neutrality, isolationism, and wealth have made them appear smug, and protective of their standard of living. In fact, their prosperity has been hard-won. They were not always rich. Proud, industrious, fair-minded, and creative, they have had a bad press.

Switzerland today is a model of peace and multicultural cooperation, yet historically the country was racked by conflict. Swiss mercenaries were a major export. The extraordinary act of will that brought together disparate social and regional groups against their common enemy in the thirteenth and fourteenth centuries was the glue that continues to hold the Confederation together today. Its decentralized political structure means that the cantons are largely autonomous, and retain their individual character. In this grassroots democracy real power lies with the people, who exercise it directly through frequent referendums. "Swissness" is, above all, a spirit of independence and of communal involvement.

In private life the Swiss are no less active and responsive. They respect the individual, which means that, while they appreciate clear thinking and direct talking, they avoid confrontation. They will never intrude, yet will willingly help out if asked. If you make the effort, you will find warmth, decency, wit, and intelligence.

*Culture Smart! Switzerland* reveals the human dimension of this enigmatic country. It provides an historical overview, explores Swiss values and attitudes, and looks at the cultural continuity of festivals and traditions. It will help you navigate your way through various aspects of Swiss life and society. There is advice on meeting people, on how to behave in different situations, and how to avoid making gaffes. It looks at the home life of the Swiss, describes what is important to them, how they work, relax, and how they perceive foreigners. And it offers crucial insights into Swiss business culture, and more generally on differences in communication style. All this will give you a starting point, to discover for yourself the many hidden riches of this fascinating society.

## Key Facts

| Official Name | *Confederatio Helveticae* (Latin), The Swiss Confederation | |
|---|---|---|
| National Names | Long forms: *Schweizerische Eidgenossenschaft* (German), *Confédération Suisse* (French), *Confederazione Svizzera* (Italian), *Confederaziun Svizra* (Romansh). Short forms: *Schweiz* (German), *La Suisse* (French), *Svizzera* (Italian), *Svizra* (Romansh). | |
| Capital City | Bern (Berne) | |
| Main Cities | Zürich, Geneva, Basel, Luzern, Lausanne, Lugano | |
| Area | 15,940 square miles (41,293 square kilometers) | |
| Climate | Temperate; varies with altitude. Cold, rainy/snowy winters; cool to warm, cloudy humid summers with occasional showers. Mediterranean in the south. | |
| Currency | Swiss franc (CHF or sFr.) | |
| Population | 7.3 million (one of the most densely populated countries in the world) | |
| Ethnic Makeup | 20.1% of the people living in Switzerland are non-Swiss. | |
| National Languages | German 63.6%; French 20.4%; Italian 6.5%; Romansh 0.5%; other 9%. | German, French, and Italian are both national and official languges. Romansh is a national language, but not official. |

| | | |
|---|---|---|
| **Religion** | Roman Catholic 41.8%; Protestant 35.2%; Muslim 4.3%; Christian Orthodox 1.8%; other Christian 0.2%; Jewish 0.2%; other churches and communities 0.8%; no affiliation 15.7%. | |
| **Government** | Federal republic of 26 cantons (23 full and 3 half-cantons). Parliament (the Federal Assembly) has two houses: the National Council and the Council of States. | The executive is the seven-member Federal Council, elected by members of parliament. The President is both head of government and head of state. |
| **Media** | The Swiss Broadcasting Corporation is a private, non-profit-making company and public service. It broadcasts in the four national languages. | Many regional and national newspapers and magazines. The *Neue Zürcher Zeitung* (German) and *Le Temps* (French) are two of the most respected. |
| **Media: English Language** | Swiss Radio International has a Web site (www.swissinfo.org) with local and English-language news available. | *Swiss News* informs Anglophones about Swiss affairs. Expatriate magazines: *Cream* (Zurich), *GEM* (Geneva). |
| **Electricity** | 220 volts, 50 Hz. | Three-pronged plugs used. Adapters needed for U.S. and British appliances. |
| **Video/TV** | PAL system | NTSC TV will not work here. |
| **Telephone** | Switzerland's country code is 41. | To dial out, dial 00. For mobiles, press + instead. |

# chapter one

# LAND & PEOPLE

Switzerland is one of the smallest countries in Europe, and one of the most densely populated. Its landmass is only 15,940 square miles (41,285 square kilometers), compared to Germany's 137,828 square miles (356,974 square kilometers) and France's 210,026 square miles (543,965 square kilometers). From north to south it measures 137 miles (220 kilometers), which takes about four hours to travel by train and three hours by car. From east to west it measures 217 miles (350 kilometers), and on any of these journeys one can see contrasting landscapes of great beauty.

The population of Switzerland is 7.3 million, and there are 176 people per square kilometer. Sixty-eight percent of the Swiss live in urban areas and 32 percent in rural.

Made up of linguistic regions that mirror the cultures of its larger neighbors, Switzerland at first glance appears to be a peculiar and artificial entity, raising the question, "How did it all come together?" Possibly this is something that the Swiss would be asking themselves today, had they not been so busy being the responsible, active, and cooperative citizens of an extremely efficiently run country. Numerous factors have played a part in the formation of this unique republic—the people themselves, the geography, and the influence of outside powers.

Switzerland evolved naturally within its own borders and continues to forge ahead on its own terms on the European continent. This is not to say that it is immune to the political currents tugging at Europe today, but it implies both a history and a positioning in the world that is founded on a certain mistrust of its neighbors. The common ground that brings the Swiss together as a people is not always clear. Perhaps the paradox of Swiss identity is best described in the saying "unity, but not uniformity." For all its diversity, Switzerland is the most stable democracy in the world today.

## CLIMATE

The climate is extremely varied. Switzerland lies at the point of intersection of the main climatic regions of Europe: the oceanic, the northern European, the Mediterranean, and the continental. Ascona, in the canton of Ticino, lies at the lowest point of the country at 643 feet (196 meters) above sea level. The climate here is much like the Mediterranean—there are even palm trees. An arctic climate is found at the country's highest point, the Dufour Peak, which is 15,199 feet (4,634 meters) high. One would have to travel only 43 miles (70 kilometers), as the crow flies, to cover the distance between these two extremes. To visitors, the country's most famous mountain,

and one of the highest in the Alps, would probably be the Matterhorn. It is situated in the south, in the canton of Valais, which is a dry, mountainous region. However, if one were to travel into the valleys of this region, one would find an abundance of apricots, cherries, tomatoes, and grapes. Temperatures in Switzerland are on average about 68°F to 77°F (20°C to 25°C) in summer and 36°F to 43°F (2°C to 6°C) in winter.

## The *Föhn*

The *Föhn*, also the German word for "hairdryer," is a warm, dry wind that swoops down over the leeward side of the Alps. It can arrive at any time of the year but occurs most frequently in spring and fall. Recognized by mostly clear skies with a distinct arch of clouds, it brings with it a quick rise in temperature and sudden atmospheric changes. These conditions are said to have an unsettling effect on people, causing headaches and anxiety. The perfect scapegoat, the *Föhn* is said to be blamed by the Swiss for all their problems.

In the French-speaking region between the Jura and the Alps a strong cold wind known as *La Bise* can blow from the north, northeast, or east in winter, spring, or fall. In winter the "*Bise Noir*" contributes to the gloom with rain, snow, or hail.

## GEOGRAPHICAL SNAPSHOT

Geographically speaking, Switzerland is divided into three regions: the Jura, the Plateau, and the Alps. The Jura (Celtic for "wood") is a limestone mountain range stretching from Lake Geneva to the Rhine and extending into eastern France and southern Germany. This subalpine area makes up about 10 percent of the country's surface area. On average, it is 2,296 feet (700 meters) above sea level. It is a picturesque highland crossed by river valleys. The rocks first studied here at the end of the eighteenth century lend their name to the Jurassic geological period.

The Plateau refers to the region between Lake Geneva and Lake Constance. With an average altitude of 1,902 feet (580 meters) and covering 30 percent of the country's surface area, it is here that one finds the majority of the population (two-thirds) as well as most of the country's industry, traffic, agriculture, and livestock.

The Alps extend over the central and southern regions of the country. These are probably the physical feature most closely associated with Swiss identity by foreign travelers. They span about 125 miles (200 kilometers) at an average altitude of 5,576 feet (1,700 meters) and cover almost two-thirds of the country's total surface area. Only 11 percent of the population live in the mountains, but 60 percent of tourism is concentrated in the Alps and their foothills. The Rhone, Upper Rhine, Reuss, and Ticino Rivers divide the mountain ranges.

The country as a whole boasts no fewer than 1,500 lakes, the largest of which are Lakes Geneva, Constance, Neuchâtel, Lucerne, Maggiore, and Zürich. It is the source of 6 percent of Europe's freshwater supply.

Switzerland has practically no natural resources. It has one of the lowest percentages of land under

cultivation in Western Europe, and overall the number of farms is dropping. Large farms, however, are on the increase. Six percent of the working population are employed in agriculture, and about one-third of the food is imported. Three-quarters of the farmed area is meadow and pasture, as most of the country is unsuitable for crops. Cereals and vegetables are grown in the lowlands. About one-third of farms are engaged in crop production. There are no large forests, but no region is without a forest either.

Because their own land is so small, the Swiss marvel at countries that take more than four or five hours' driving time to traverse. In some cases, they almost seem to apologize for their own. They take for granted the scale of their magnificent mountains and the diversity of the countryside— you only need travel for an hour or two to experience different cultures, languages, traditions, architecture, scenery, even countries.

### *A Sense of Scale*

North Americans in particular need to adjust their notions of proximity and distance in Switzerland. Out for a drive through the countryside, a hapless American commented after about thirty to forty minutes, "Hey, the Zürich area is really beautiful," which thoroughly put out his Swiss girlfriend. They had, after all, passed through three or four different cantons by this time and were now in a totally different part of the country, practically at the border with Germany. The American concluded: Don't blink, or you may miss a canton; and pay attention to the "Welcome to Canton . . ." signs to keep track of where you are.

## LANGUAGES

Since 1937 there have been four national languages in Switzerland: German, French, Italian, and Romansh (the closest living descendant of ancient Latin). Of these, German, French, and Italian are official languages. They enjoy equal status in Parliament, the federal administration, and the army. Because it is not one of the official languages, all laws do not have to be translated into Romansh. While each linguistic region has close ties with its neighboring country, these relationships are somewhat ambivalent. The Swiss display as much rejection of a neighboring culture as affinity with it, because it appears to pose a threat to Swiss identity. The federal census in 2000 produced the following picture of how the language groups are divided: German 63.6 percent, French 20.4 percent, Italian 6.5 percent, Romansh 0.5 percent, other 9 percent.

Schools have played a key role in bringing the people closer together, with every child learning a second national language from his or her seventh year at the latest. However, when it was decided in 2004 that Swiss children should learn two extra languages at school, the German cantons gave priority to English as the second language, rather than French or Italian. This step has not been well received by the minority Swiss communities.

## The German-Speaking Region

This is the largest language region, and was for a long time a mosaic of urban and rural areas with a profusion of very distinct Alemannic dialects, which still exist today. The German-speaking Swiss learn their cultivated official language, High German, at school; they call it "written German," and it always retains an element of strangeness for them. In normal speech they use an unwritten everyday language, which varies greatly from region to region. The grammar and vowels of these dialects, known by the collective term

*Schwyzerdütsch*, or Swiss German, can be traced back to Middle High German. They have produced their own literature since the nineteenth century. National radio and television allow the dialects plenty of scope, and they are also used to a certain extent in churches and schools.

### The French-Speaking Region

The second national language is spoken in the cantons of Geneva, Jura, Neuchâtel, and Vaud, as well as in parts of the cantons of Bern, Fribourg, and Valais. Called *Romandie* by the French Swiss and *Westschweiz* by the German, the French-speaking region also used to have its dialects, but the Church and schools suppressed them in the rural districts. The French spoken in western Switzerland has some regional characteristics, but otherwise its citizens speak French as it is spoken in France.

The Protestant teachings of the Geneva-based reformer Jean Calvin played a decisive role in shaping the cultural identity of these cantons, even though not all the French Swiss are Protestant.

### The Italian-Speaking Region

Italian is spoken in the southern valleys up to the St. Gotthard, Lukmanier, and San Bernardino passes. This region comprises the whole of the canton of Ticino (or Tessin in French and German) and the valleys of Misox/Calanca, Bergell/Bregaglia, and Poschiavo in the canton of Graubünden (also known as the Grisons). Although the construction and development of international traffic routes (such as the St. Gotthard Pass) and tourism from the north have brought an economic upswing to this previously relatively impoverished southern part of Switzerland, they have also resulted in a threat to the region's cultural identity.

The rich local dialects remain intact in rural areas, whereas artists and writers tend to look toward nearby Milan, the cultural center of northern Italy.

### The Romansh-Speaking Region

The valleys of Rhaetia (today's Graubünden) were conquered in 15 BCE by the Romans, and this resulted in the latinization of the original inhabitants. The isolation of the numerous valleys led to the development of at least five distinct language forms—a unique linguistic phenomenon in such a small area—each with its own written tradition and each with several dialects. But in recent years the influx of tourists and migration to the economic centers of German-speaking Switzerland have threatened to erode this linguistic idyll. Endeavors, such as the creation of a single written language in 1982 known as *rumantsch grischun*, have been made to try to stop the process of erosion, for administrative as well as cultural reasons.

In the nature of things, the smaller language groups often have to struggle to assert their poltical and economic influence.

## A BRIEF HISTORY

In the first millennium BCE the early warlike inhabitants of Switzerland were overrun by more sophisticated Celtic tribes from the west, in particular the Helvetians and the Rhaetians, who occupied the country from about 400 BCE to 400 CE. The Romans began their conquest around 107 BCE. Under Julius Caesar, in 58 BCE, and later under the Emperor Augustus, they consolidated their control over the Gauls (their name for the Celts) and proceeded to move further north into what is now Germany, but were forced back. The Rhine became the border of the Roman Empire and remained so until the first years of the fifth century.

The Celtic population was soon assimilated

into Roman civilization, and the Romans presided over two centuries of peace and prosperity, building roads, founding towns, and opening up the country to trade. The names of numerous mountains, rivers, and places are reminders of the Helvetic and Roman past.

This tranquillity came to an end in 260 CE when Aleman invaders from north of the Rhine broke through the imperial defenses and settled in the Swiss Plateau in such large numbers that their language, the ancestor of Swiss German, drove out the local tongue. The Germanic peoples of northern and eastern Europe were on the move, pushed westward by tribes migrating from Central Asia. When Rome finally withdrew its forces in around 400 CE, the Germanic tribes took control. In the west, the Burgundian settlers adopted Christianity and the Latin language, and in the Alpine valleys of the south the Lombardic and Romansh peoples maintained their cultural ties with Rome. This marked the beginning of the language divide in Switzerland.

Christianity, introduced by the Romans, spread and the Church became a major landowner and temporal power. From the sixth century, the Franks, also a Germanic people, gradually moved in from the west, bringing first the Burgundians, then later the Alemans, under their rule. Two successive Frankish dynasties—the Merovingians and the Carolingians—presided over a lengthy period of peace, culminating in the reign of Charlemagne. His Frankish empire reinforced Latin Christianity, created a network of monasteries, and introduced the feudal system, by which landed nobles exercised direct political power over the people on their estates. There was no "state" to speak of during this period; the warrior noble classes accumulated power through conquest, inheritance, and marriage, and the Roman towns declined.

The breakup of Charlemagne's empire after his death ushered in a period of conflict and instability. Order was eventually restored in the eleventh century under the Holy Roman Empire, when Switzerland was controlled by a number of ruling dynasties, including the house of Habsburg.

At the end of the Middle Ages, from the ninth to the fourteenth century, Europe experienced a general rise in temperature—it was 1.5 to 2.25 degrees warmer than today. The warmer climate, coupled with improved farming techniques, led to an increase in agricultural production, which was able to support a growing population. By the eleventh century the social and economic consequences of this new prosperity were starting to be felt in Switzerland. There was a resurgence of urban life that continued into the twelfth and thirteenth centuries. The period saw the emergence of guilds of specialized craftsmen, the rise of a wealthy merchant class, and the building of roads across the Alps. In  particular, the opening up of a trade route to the Mediterranean and beyond through the St. Gotthard Pass in 1230 had a huge impact on the country.

## The Swiss Confederation

In the twelfth and thirteenth centuries the papacy and the Holy Roman Empire competed for supremacy in Europe. The Emperorship was elective, and was hotly contested when the position fell vacant. At the same time the feudal system was starting to break down. Various princes or kings were reducing the powerful feudal lords to royal obedience, leading to the rise of independent national kingdoms, which in turn reduced the authority of the Empire.

In the absence of firm government, many local communities took over the functions of the state, seeking protection and creating order themselves. In Switzerland, peasants had cleared and settled otherwise unproductive mountain areas that were of little interest to the local nobility. As a result these regions became virtually self-governing, answerable only to the Emperor himself. The rural communes of Uri, Schwyz, and Unterwalden, which together constructed the St. Gotthard Pass, were three such territories.

Elsewhere in Europe the development of local autonomy was ended by the rising power of the great ruling dynasties. In Switzerland alone a unique alliance of townsfolk and peasants helped to maintain the autonomous commune, thus defining the nature of the future Swiss state. Even today the commune, or *Gemeinde*, is a vital part of the Swiss political system.

The Habsburgs were by now one of Europe's leading dynasties. Rudolf I of Habsburg was elected Holy Roman Emperor in 1273, and used his position to acquire the archduchy of Austria as a hereditary possession. He consolidated his power in Austria and sent bailiffs into Uri, Schwyz, and Unterwalden, which had not been subject to overlords in the past, to administer them on behalf of the Empire. On his death in 1291 rebellions broke out across the country. The three forest communities, fearing further encroachments on their liberty, joined together in a defensive alliance. In 1291, on the Rütli meadow by Lake Lucerne, they swore an oath of mutual support by which each undertook to help the others against anyone trying to subjugate them. This compact is regarded as the birth of the Swiss Confederation. It did not propose disobedience to the overlords, but it categorically rejected the imposition of any outside administrative or judicial system. It guaranteed the peaceful settlement of all disputes, the provision of legal aid, and the acceptance of binding arbitration. Foreign bailiffs were to be resisted. This pivotal event gave rise to the legend of William Tell, the heroic countryman who defied Habsburg rule. Whether historical truth or mythical creation, it has come to epitomize Swiss pride and independence.

The Swiss Confederates had not seen the last of the Habsburgs, however. The armies of the new Emperor Ludwig of Habsburg set out from Austria to reclaim the territories and rights lost to the Empire. At the Battle of Morgarten in 1315, the Austrian knights were roundly defeated by the Swiss peasants, and on the heels of this pivotal victory, over the next forty years, other communities would join the Confederation.

## *THE STORY OF WILLIAM TELL*

Canton Uri was crucial to the Habsburgs for control of the transalpine trade. Soon after the cantons of Uri, Schwyz, and Unterwalden had signed the oath of allegiance at the Rütli meadow pledging to resist Austrian oppression, the Emperor sent a bailiff, Hermann Gessler, to Altdorf in Uri. Gessler raised a pole in the central square, perched his hat on top of it, and commanded all who passed to bow in respect.

Soon matters came to a head. William Tell, a countryman from nearby Bürglen, either out of ignorance or in sheer defiance of the command, walked past the hat without bowing. Tell, who had a reputation as a fine marksman, was seized by Gessler and presented with a challenge. He ordered him to shoot an apple off his son's head with his crossbow. If Tell was successful, Gessler would release him. If he refused, both he and his son would die. Legend has it that Tell selected two arrows; one he put in his quiver, the other in his crossbow. He then took aim and shot the apple clear off his son's head. Impressed but infuriated, Gessler had to ask what the second arrow was for. Tell looked him in the eye and told him that if the first arrow had struck his boy, the second would have been for Gessler. For this insolence, Tell was arrested and sentenced to lifelong imprisonment in the dungeons of Gessler's castle at Küssnacht, northeast of Lake Lucerne.

On the way to Küssnacht, a violent storm disoriented the oarsmen. They begged Gessler to untie Tell, who was familiar with the lake, so that he could steer them safely to shore. When Gessler agreed to the request, Tell maneuvered the boat close to the shore and managed to escape. Still armed with his second arrow, Tell hurried to Küssnacht, where he killed Gessler on his way to the castle. Upon his return to Uri, he served as inspiration to his comrades to remain free and independent from foreign rule.

## The Roots of Neutrality

After the victory of the Swiss cantons over the Swabian League in 1498, the Emperor Maximilian I was forced to grant them *de facto* independence. Confederate expansion seemed unstoppable until the battle of Marignano, where the cantons faced the combined might of the French and the Venetians. The Confederates lost and this ended their military expansion forever. It was also the beginning of Swiss neutrality. Since 1515 Switzerland has followed the injunction of its hermit prophet, Nicholas con der Flüe: "Don't build your fences too far out!"

By the sixteenth century there were thirteen cantons in the Confederation, all technically under the suzerainty of the Holy Roman Empire, but in practice independent republics bound together by defensive treaties. The member cities and states were without a strong central government. The Confederation was also split equally between Catholics and Protestants. For these reasons it was very difficult to forge a common foreign policy. Added to this, the promise of mutual protection that was part of the oath of 1291 helped to define an inner power balance that made it impossible to take sides in the surrounding conflict. Switzerland remained neutral in the wars of religion that swept across Europe in the wake of the Protestant Reformation.

Despite its neutrality, foreign Protestant forces twice invaded the country, in 1633 and 1638. The Confederation Diet responded by setting up a joint military council, made up of Protestant and Catholic members, charged with providing a force of 36,000 armed men to guard the borders. This new arrangement was known as the "*Defensionale von Wil*" ("Defense Charter of Will"). At the end of the Thirty Years War in 1648, in which Switzerland played no part, the Confederation's independence was finally recognized by the Holy Roman Empire, and the policy of neutrality was formalized.

Switzerland has been called a *Willensnation*, a nation created by the will of the people, that otherwise has no uniform ethnic or religious identity. This concept, while strengthened after the Thirty Years War, was established much earlier during the Reformation.

### The Reformation

Switzerland was home to two of Europe's leading Protestant reformers, one in the German-speaking area, the other in the French. Ulrich Zwingli was rector and teacher of religion at the Great Minster in Zürich. He preached the ideal of a Christian commonwealth, advocating the separation of the Church from the state, while calling on the state authorities to model their laws on the laws of God. The city of Zürich embraced the Reformation in 1523, and Zwingli worked energetically to spread its ideas on Swiss soil. His militant attempts to reorganize the Confederation under the leadership of Protestant Zürich and Bern alienated many rural Catholics, however, and he was killed in a battle against the Catholic cantons in 1531.

The reformist theologian John (Jean) Calvin sought asylum in Basel after breaking with the Catholic Church in his native France. His *Institutes of the Christian Religion*, a justification of the principles of the Reformation, was to have as profound an influence on the Reformation as Martin Luther's Bible. Like Luther he believed in the primacy of Scripture, but, more than Luther, he believed in predestination. He argued that a strict moral code was the basis for Christian life, and that a properly constituted religious and secular authority should not be challenged. After his appointment as city preacher in Geneva, Calvin attempted to establish a form of theocracy there, but he was driven out by a popular revolt in 1538. Recalled to Geneva in 1541, he succeeded in restructuring the state to establish the supremacy of the Church. His theocratic government, "the most perfect school of Christ," became a focal point for the defense of Protestantism throughout Europe, and grew increasingly intolerant of religious dissent, even burning one heretic at the stake. He founded the University of Geneva, and successfully exported his ideas to distant lands.

The Reformation in Switzerland threatened the alliance of the thirteen Confederates. The larger towns like Zürich, Basel, Bern, Neuchâtel, and Geneva embraced Protestantism, while the conservative rural areas in central Switzerland (one-third of the population) remained Roman Catholic. In an age when religion was the greatest force for the unification or separation of peoples, Switzerland's neighbors were almost all Catholic. The antagonism between the Swiss Protestants and their Catholic neighbors in the German lands widened the breach between the Confederation and the Empire.

Within Switzerland religious disputes continued in the Villmergen Wars of 1656 and 1712, in which the Catholic cantons were drawn into a temporary alliance with France. As a country constructed on its own terms, however, Switzerland held fast to the principles upon which it was founded—not to be controlled by another power—and its people eventually chose religious tolerance at a time when the nation could have broken apart.

**The Foundations of Modern Switzerland**

In 1798 the armies of Revolutionary France invaded Switzerland and Napoleon created the Helvetic Republic. His attempt to impose a centralized, French system of government on the Swiss, doing away with autonomous cantons, met with universal opposition. In 1803 the Mediation Act was passed, sanctioning the principle of a federal system embracing the nineteen existing cantons. France's jurisdiction in Switzerland lasted until Napoleon's defeat at Waterloo in 1815. The legacy of the Helvetic Republic was the promotion of an ideal that remains fundamental to Swiss society—pursuit of the common good. The Swiss rejected both the French model of the centralized state, and the opposition of their own wealthy oligarchs to the greater empowerment of the people. The republican and federalist forces that opposed Napoleon's centralizing policy created a strong bond between people and regions very different from one another.

The tide of liberalism and nationalism unleashed by the French swept across Europe.

In the 1840s, radical liberals in the Protestant cantons broke up the "Sonderbünd"—a defensive association of seven Catholic cantons—and forced them to adopt liberal constitutions, expel religious orders, and join in a closer union of all the Swiss cantons. The 1848 constitution gave the country a more centralized government and created further economic cohesion. In the following decades the peculiarly Swiss form of direct democracy, characterized by frequent referendums, took shape, and in 1874 a revised constitution established the principle that if enough citizens demanded it, all new legislation could be put to a nationwide vote. This remains a cornerstone of the Swiss political system today.

With political stability came economic and social stability. The nineteenth century was a time of considerable industrial growth. Poor in natural resources, the country began to develop precision industries dependent on highly skilled labor. It is no accident that Switzerland is today renowned for its watches. Railways and roads were built, opening up Alpine areas to tourism, and new commercial banks were established.

The International Red Cross was founded by Swiss businessman and humanitarian Henri Dunant after he wrote a memoir about his travels to Italy, and specifically to the site of the battle of Solferino, where the French had defeated the

Austrians. He was stunned by the number of soldiers wounded and left to die, and advocated the establishment of an international network of volunteer relief agencies. His book was noticed by the Swiss Federal Council, and in 1863 it sponsored an international conference to discuss ways of implementing Dunant's ideas. In 1864 twelve countries ratified the document that became the basis for the International Committee of the Red Cross and the first Geneva Convention. Dunant was a corecipient of the first Nobel Peace Prize, awarded in 1901, along with French economist and advocate of international arbitration, Frederic Passy.

## GOVERNMENT

The Swiss Federation has twenty-six sovereign cantons—twenty-three full cantons and three half-cantons (for example, Basel-Stadt and Basel-

Land). The chief of state and head of government is the president. The bicameral national parliament, the Federal Assembly, consists of an upper chamber called the Council of States, which represents the cantons with forty-six seats, two per canton (one per half canton), and a lower chamber, the National Council, whose delegates represent the people directly, with two hundred seats allocated to the cantons in proportion to the size of their populations. Each canton gets at least one. The Federal Assembly elects seven members to form a cabinet, the Federal Council, which holds executive power. All offices are for a four-year term, but the president and vice president are rotated annually and the title is largely ceremonial. The Federal Council operates on a congenial principle whereby whatever decision is adopted, all must stand unanimously behind it. Consequently there is no official opposition. The most direct of democracies, the Swiss system is characterized by referendums. If enough signatures (fifty thousand) are gathered on a particular issue, it can go to a vote.

The Federal Council has adhered to a "magic formula" since 1959, which has been a power-sharing arrangement between the top four parties. This changed recently, following the October 2003 parliamentary elections, marking a clear shift to the right when the Swiss People's Party gained another seat, causing the Christian People's Party to drop to a single seat, and shifting the balance of power for the first time in forty-four years.

The smallest political entities in Switzerland, the three thousand *Gemeinden/Communes*, are an integral part of the Swiss system. They have their own elected administration, and, depending on the community, citizens cast a ballot or participate more directly by gathering in town assemblies where issues are voted upon.

## FOREIGN POLICY

Switzerland is obliged by its constitution to be neutral in any conflict between other nations. This policy of staying out of international disputes arose from its historical lack of centralized leadership. After the fall of Napoleon, Swiss neutrality was formally recognized and guaranteed by the great powers of Europe in 1815 at the Vienna conference on international affairs. Thus it was that Switzerland took no active part in either of the two world wars. Without that neutrality, during the First World War, the country might well have fallen apart, with the French Swiss following the French and the German Swiss the Germans. This was not the case in the Second World War. Switzerland has recently come under severe criticism for its role during the war, when it did little to help Jewish refugees and accepted gold from the Nazis that was known to have been stolen from Jews.

After voting against joining the United Nations in 1986, when 75 percent of Swiss voters rejected the proposal on the grounds that it would compromise their neutrality, they reconsidered in

March 2003, opting to join. This is a good demonstration of the "slow but sure" Swiss way of doing things—it took fifteen years to retable the issue after it had been decided by the people. The Swiss delegation drove home the point that although Switzerland was one of the last nations to join, it was the first to do so as a result of direct democracy. Ironically the European headquarters of the U.N. have been in Geneva since 1945.

> "Switzerland is a vivid example of what the U.N. stands for—a peaceful and multicultural society built on strong democratic foundations."
> *Kofi Annan*

In 1992 the French Swiss voted for a proposal to join the European Union, but were overruled by the German Swiss, who declined to join for both economic and national reasons (they would have become a minority group within the larger German-speaking European population). Direct democracy and the Swiss spirit of independence have been the driving forces against E.U. membership.

In 2001 the Swiss again rejected the people's initiative entitled "Yes to Europe!" However, this result does not amount to an outright rejection of the E.U. Never prone to jump in hastily, the Swiss are seeking an assurance that particular preconditions for negotiations first be met. Certain bilateral agreements, which took four years to negotiate, have already been signed, and their implementation is a top priority. Discussion on a second package of agreements is under way.

Despite Switzerland's hesitation over joining the major world bodies, it has strong political and economic ties with the rest of the world and is a member of various international organizations. The Swiss economy is export driven and relies upon the international market. One in every two Swiss francs is earned abroad. Three-fifths of Switzerland's exports are to the E.U. while four-fifths of its imports come from there.

In 1960, Switzerland was a founding member of the European Free Trade Association (EFTA); in 1963 it joined the European Council, and in 1975 the Organization for Security and Cooperation in Europe (OSCE). It is also a member of the Organization for Economic Cooperation and Development (OECD). Switzerland has been a member of the World Bank and the International Monetary Fund since 1992.

## THE SWISS PEOPLE TODAY

The Swiss take great pride in their system of direct democracy, humanitarian tradition, and political neutrality, but are today challenged to redefine themselves in a changing world. As Europe's borders soften, remaining a special case is not as easy or practical as it once appeared. The rise of the far right is as real in Switzerland as in its European neighbors, the high number of foreign refugees and asylum seekers continues to grow, and the Swiss are finding that their old certainties are no longer serving them so well.

It is common on the streets of major Swiss cities to hear not only English being spoken, but the languages, for example, of Kosovo and North Africa. In villages set in idyllic scenery, next to million-dollar homes, live refugees in cramped, temporary housing. Integration of this immigrant population, through programs such as language education, is a priority for government and aid agencies alike, but most refugees still live in isolation from the community around them. Unable to work, and with very little money, they are both marginalized and blamed for increasing crime rates, as they await verdicts on their asylum applications (which can take months). Confronted by this influx, Swiss people of all political persuasions are having to reexamine traditional values and long-held beliefs. What is best for the common good is anything but straightforward or clear. Cohesiveness has never been a prerequisite for the success of this country. In the atmosphere of Europe today, the Swiss may have to work that much harder to overcome today's challenges.

## CITIES

In a 2004  survey of the quality of life in two hundred and fifteen countries—based on thirty-nine criteria, including political, social, economic, and environmental factors, personal safety, and health, education, transportation, and other public services—Zürich was rated the best city in the world, Geneva second, and Bern sixth. Switzerland's cities are not characterized by dominating skylines, or even large city centers. Instead, the centers of even the biggest cities have a small-town atmosphere. The larger Swiss cities are actually sprawling conurbations embracing smaller outlying suburbs.

The autonomy of each *Gemeinde/Commune* not only allows for a relatively high degree of involvement in political life on the part of its citizens, but actually makes it necessary. Switzerland has historically maintained a great deal of respect for the independence of its smallest political unit, and local government allows each city suburb and community to be the germ cell of a markedly pluralistic society. This degree of local autonomy helps explain the reluctance of the Swiss to join the E.U.—they don't want to lose it.

The capital and seat of government is the medieval city of Bern (Berne). It was here, while working in the Swiss Patent Office, that Albert Einstein developed the theory of relativity. Bern is also famous as the home of Toblerone chocolate and Emmental cheese—Swiss cheese to the rest of the world.

Zürich is Switzerland's largest city and is an important center for international finance, industry, and commerce. Regarded as rather arrogant by the other Swiss cities, it is also considered particularly receptive to contemporary trends, has the largest number of museums, and

hosts many exhibitions. It promotes itself as "Zürich, downtown Switzerland."

The small town of Winterthur, only fifteen minutes from Zürich, supports a vibrant music and theater scene.

Basel (Basle), a river port on the Rhine, lies on the borders of France and Germany. It is home to the chemical and pharmaceutical industries. Its university was founded by Pope Pius II in 1460, and the city was a center of Humanist scholarship. Holbein established his reputation there. Erasmus lived there from 1521 until the introduction of the Reformation in 1529. The city today has a thriving music and jazz scene.

Luzern (Lucerne), situated on the beautiful lake of the same name, is home to the popular Swiss Transport Museum and known for quaint and lively cafés and boutiques.

Zug is a tax haven and many multinational companies are registered there.

Chur is said to have the best shopping between Zürich and Milan. It is old, and full of character.

The completely bilingual city of Biel/Bienne is the watch-making center of Switzerland, where Omega and Rolex are based.

Fribourg/Freiburg is a medieval town with a modern heart, and is an amiable and easy-going place. It is known for its bilingual (French/German) university.

Geneva (Genève), birthplace of Calvinism, and of Jean Jacques Rousseau, is Switzerland's second-largest city. It is the headquarters of over two hundred international organizations, including the European headquarters of the United Nations, the International Red Cross, and the World Health Organization.

Lausanne, on the northern shore of Lake Geneva, is said to be the most beautiful city in Switzerland. It is home to the international Olympic museum, and also supports a large counterculture (by Swiss standards).

Neuchâtel is notable as the city with the best French in Switzerland (many foreigners go to learn French there). It is also the base of many multinational corporations.

If it weren't for the world-famous annual jazz festival that takes place there every year, Montreux, at the eastern end of Lake Geneva, might be considered rather dull, but it is, of course, beautiful. Because of its exceptional microclimate, it is known as "the Riviera."

Bulle, according to an internal Swiss survey, has the best quality of life in French Switzerland.

Lugano is an energetic and stylish resort on Lake Lugano, in the Italian part of the country, which hasn't become as "touristy" as its counterpart on Lake Maggiore, Locarno, which hosts the annual open-air film festival.

# chapter two

# VALUES & ATTITUDES

## UNITY NOT UNIFORMITY

Swiss history demonstrates that the often divisive forces of language and religion don't have to stand in the way of building a successful, democratic nation-state. This is evident today when taking a closer look at the country's geopolitical structure. The borders of the cantons often mark religious and linguistic areas, and most were created with either a Protestant or a Catholic majority. There are regions where, as a result of religious, social, or economic differences, two communities divided a single territory between them to form "half cantons." In fact, the newest full canton, Jura, was formed when it split from Canton Bern in 1979. By and large, however, the map of Switzerland is one drawn with tolerant hands, yet molded with expectations of conformity—a contradiction, perhaps, but a working formula for the most stable and efficient country in the world. So what lies behind the phrase, "Unity not Uniformity," and what influence does it have on the culture of the Swiss people?

## RESPONSIBLE CITIZENS

The country and its people are characteristically efficient, honest, and extremely law-abiding citizens, even though they live under a highly decentralized system of government that in theory places great power of opposition in their hands. What makes the country work may be just the fact that its citizens are not interested in the concept of centralized government or a powerful head of state. History and the doctrine of the "common good" implemented by the reformers Calvin and Zwingli have contributed to a political system that places trust in the responsible nature of individuals. Being a nation does not preoccupy people. Doing their part, in their part of the country, is what holds the nation together. Not overtly patriotic (even though the Swiss flag is ubiquitous), the Swiss are nevertheless extremely proud of the system of direct democracy that gives them "*Sonderfall*" or "special case" status on the world scene.

You might therefore presume that the average Swiss is an eager citizen anxious to take advantage of his democratic rights. This is not particularly the case. A 30 percent turnout at the polls is par for the course; turnout is much higher for major issues such as E.U. membership or the initiative to abolish the Swiss army. However, the responsible nature of the Swiss, if not seen at the polls, is clear on a personal level in the great respect and tolerance they have for friends, neighbors, and colleagues. Rousseau, in the eighteenth century, instilled this democratic mindset by pointing out that a person's freedom, valuable as it is, can only go as far as where the next person's freedom begins.

## SOCIAL CONTROL

Somewhat like the noisy Irish family in London who gave English the term "Hooligan," the family name Bünzli provides the Swiss with a name that epitomizes "Swissness." "Bünzli" can be summed up in the word conformist, even boring; someone who always does the correct thing and never rebels. Hardly a hooligan, but you get the point.

Obeying the rules goes, for the most part, unquestioned in Swiss culture. The Swiss even hold referendums, on average eight times a year, to improve the social system. In general, they do what makes sense, and not adhering to a particular law would only jeopardize the workings of an efficient society. An example of this can be seen on any given day when people dutifully bring their standard garbage bags, cardboard, newspapers, compost, old furniture, aluminium, plastic bottles, and glass, and deposit them in the appropriate place for recycling. Although you are rarely checked for a ticket on the tram, people obediently buy their tickets each and every time. Youths have been seen to go astray, putting their feet on the adjacent seat, but not before dutifully placing a newspaper under their muddy shoes! It's not uncommon to see drivers turning off the ignition while waiting at train crossings or stoplights or anywhere that waiting could exceed thirty seconds, in order to cut down on exhaust emissions. In the 1970s and '80s special advertisements were set up at traffic lights exhorting drivers to turn off their engines.

Leaving nothing to chance, however, the Swiss make sure there is an ample number of rules to ensure things run smoothly. In German Switzerland, for example, if you haven't adequately recycled, and your garbage bags are brimming and numerous, you'll suffer financial consequences. Each plastic garbage bag comes with a hefty price tag in order to keep usage down, and if you use an improper bag, "garbage police" sort through your trash looking for clues to your name or address, and impose a huge 100 Swiss francs fine for illegal dumping. The country has also set car exhaust control standards that are the strictest in Europe, and all cars must pass yearly exhaust emission tests. The environment is obviously a great concern and a priority for the

Swiss, but it is also symbolic of the common good that they so responsibly look after. Because Switzerland is so small, people have to live next to the garbage and pollution they produce. Likewise, they have to live with one another's behavior.

## A SELF-POLICING SOCIETY

A sense of duty, which is similarly seen in their neighbors the Germans, runs deep in Swiss culture. Correct behavior is expected, and if police seem few and far between, don't be fooled; the Swiss themselves are quick to point out where you've failed in your obligations. Whether you've squeezed your minivan into a compact car-parking space or tried to evade taxes, don't assume that someone observing this will see it as none of his business. With so many people in such a small space, the Swiss have developed ways of getting along. This makes them seem severe, and life downright miserable. Without a doubt, pressure to be proper looms large, but if you respect the responsible nature of Switzerland's citizens, it is easier not to take the looks and occasional reprimands (usually from the elderly) so personally, and to recognize that these don't come from ill intent.

There is a flipside to living in such a law-abiding society. Because of this innate sense of personal responsibility, it is often possible to find places where you can buy items on the honor system. In the French part of the country you deposit your money into the box of a newspaper dispenser. On the outskirts of cities or in rural areas, you can pick flowers or buy fruit and vegetables, firewood, jams, milk, and yogurt simply by dropping coins in a bucket. It should be mentioned, however, that more recently it's not uncommon to see small surveillance cameras in place—just in case.

As important as social control to the Swiss is their respect for others' boundaries. It is only when the "common good" is undermined that the Swiss display their sense of duty and override their reluctance to push those boundaries. Switzerland provides a breath of fresh air for celebrities, or people of notoriety, who are looking for privacy. The Swiss would never feel it was their place to invade the space of someone famous by approaching him or her for an autograph or a piece of the limelight. This is also indicative of how they treat one another. There is a well-defined line between what is private and what is not, and personal space is generally honored. This attitude pervades several realms, including friendship and the workplace, and will be discussed in later chapters.

### KLARTEXT (CLARITY)

The Swiss like to "say it like it is." They don't mince words and would never cushion constructive criticism with praise. To a foreigner, this can seem a bit harsh, but it is not meant to be taken personally. Their "*Klartext*" does not imply a definitive statement but one that is open for discussion, and opinion is welcome. The Swiss are adaptable and their directness does not preclude compromise; its aim is to achieve accuracy rather than one-upmanship.

Their penchant for directness may cause inner conflict in some situations, as the Swiss are naturally nonconfrontational. They might well remain silent rather than disagree openly, in order to avoid conflict. This striving for a shared goal permeates Swiss culture. Consensus is the key.

The Latins are just as outspoken as the German Swiss, but tend to be more emollient in their manner. The French Swiss, generally speaking, are better conversationalists than the German, who have a difficult time with small talk and never stray far from the business at hand.

> "I consider looseness with words
> no less of a defect than looseness
> of the bowels."
> *Jean Calvin*

## TRANSPARENCY AND SECRECY

In the wake of the scandals of Enron, World Com, and others, much of the developed world is working toward "good governance" and "transparency." However, if you want to maintain a positive relationship with your Swiss colleagues, never question Switzerland's bank secrecy laws (which are currently slated for integration into the constitution). The Swiss see themselves as the custodians of privacy and personal liberty. The key to their propriety, they will assure you, is that the banks have strict guidelines and requirements for accepting new deposits, clients, etc. This may be true, but it all happens behind closed doors.

Swiss bank secrecy laws have protected customers' funds for over three hundred years. The first major foreign clients were the kings of France. The bankers in Geneva in the eighteenth century were actually Protestants, many of whom had fled France following the Revocation of the Edict of Nantes by Louis XIV in 1685. Discretion about the financing of the French King by heretic Protestants was, of course, in the interest of all involved.

The earliest secrecy legislation dates to 1713, when the cantonal council of Geneva adopted regulations obliging bankers to "Keep a register of their clientele and their transactions. They are, however, prohibited from divulging this information to anyone other than the client concerned, except with expressed agreement of the City Council." From these early times, Switzerland became a safe haven, not only politically but also financially for those fleeing upheaval. Bank secrecy was regulated by Swiss civil law.

The policy of client protection was later reinforced in the face of threats and pressure from Switzerland's closest neighbors, Germany and France. In 1932, the radical austerity program of the Herriot government in France called for legal control over two thousand French-owned accounts in Switzerland. The French Left supported this measure against tax avoidance, while the French Right opposed state interference in the private sphere. The Swiss held fast to their banking laws to protect client confidentiality.

In 1933, after the German Nazi government decreed that any German national with foreign capital would be punished by death, the Gestapo began spying on Swiss banks. After three Germans were executed for having an account in Switzerland, the Swiss authorities determined to protect bank clients by the criminal code.

To demonstrate its independence and neutrality, in 1934 the Swiss federal parliament passed a law that made violation of bank secrecy a criminal offense, punishable by imprisonment of the banker, fines, and the payment of damages. Exceptions to this involve matters such as drug trafficking or gun smuggling. In 1984, the people of Switzerland voted overwhelmingly in favor of maintaining bank secrecy.

## LANGUAGE AND IDENTITY

It is common to hear Canadians say of their national identity that they don't have one; or "We are not American." Similarly, the Swiss don't have a coherent identity but one made up of several linguistic and cultural strands. Switzerland does not, however, have the "melting pot" mentality predominant in North America. Instead, they've managed to keep all burners simmering, maintaining a nation of varying tastes. Whatever their linguistic background, all the regions share in the pride of their "*sonderfall*" or "special case" status within Europe. After all, with the original oath signed in 1291, the three original cantons swore that they would never be ruled by anyone but a fellow countryman. This does not imply, however, that regional identities are ambiguous. On the contrary, they are well defined and diverse, and make Switzerland and what binds it all together that much more interesting.

The downside of this strong sense of regional identity is what the Swiss themselves call "*Kantönligeischt*," or the small-minded spirit of local self-interest.

*Röstigraben*

The "*Röstigraben*"—or "*Rösti*" divide—is a term used to explain the differences between the French- and German-speaking Swiss. *Rösti* is a traditional dish of shredded potatoes, with or without cheese and bacon, which, although eaten by everyone today, originated in the German parts. The *Röstigraben* symbolizes not only a difference of language but also of values and attitudes, and its roots go back to the creation of the country itself. The original cantons were German-speaking, and some French-speaking cantons were annexed by the German Swiss.

Today it is commonly felt that the French and Italian Swiss have a bit of a minority complex in relation to their German-speaking compatriots. They wouldn't necessarily say this themselves, but the reality is that the Latin-speaking population must deal with a general attitude that to be successful in Switzerland you have to be German Swiss, and that all the money, work, and industry is in the German part of the country. The St. Gallen business school, in the German region, is considered the management pool of Switzerland, and to make it there you must speak perfect German. Politically speaking, even though a strong federal system delegates power to the smallest of cantons, the majority German-speaking population is able to decide the future of the country. Thus, the French Swiss voted unequivocally to join the E.U. more than ten years ago, but the German Swiss, who are in the majority, voted against joining, and the French were overruled. This result was not swallowed easily by the French.

It is also worth mentioning that the French Swiss have a major problem with the German language, as they learn only High German or "*Hochdeutsch*" at school and are lost as soon as they have to deal with "*Schwyzerdütsch*." Likewise, the German Swiss do not much like speaking High German.

The whole scene deteriorates even further as neither the French Swiss nor the German Swiss are fluent or even comfortable using the Italian language. During preparations for a national exposition held in Switzerland in 2002, the Italian Swiss were deeply offended when the organizing committee sent a team to make a presentation in Ticino, and none of the team members spoke Italian!

### Local Dialect

Dialect is important to the Swiss, who seem to forgo strong national pride in favor of being identified with the community from which they come. This is particularly the case in the German Swiss regions where there are as many Swiss German dialects as cantons. For example, the *Züridütsch* of Zürich is recognizably different from the *Baseldytsch* of Basel, and the moment people open their mouths, it is apparent from which canton they come.

### Language Barriers

A French Swiss woman spent a year in Germany learning High German. When she arrived in Zürich to work in a Swiss bank, she was told that the team members weren't willing to speak High German just for her. Finally, she returned to the French part of Switzerland because she couldn't cope with this attitude, or with the *Züridütsch*.

### Voting Patterns

The cultural differences between the language groups can be seen in their voting patterns. Generally voters in the Romandie and Tessin are more left wing than the German-speakers. They are more critical of the army and more in favor of state intervention in business than the Germans. In Francophone regions road traffic surcharges have no chance of being voted in, and French-speakers generally vote against regulation in areas such as the protection of animals and the environment.

That said, there is broad agreement among the liberal left across language groups on matters such as equal rights for women, abortion, and treatment for sexual offenders. Here the vote tends to be divided along urban and rural lines, with the cities voting for and the countryfolk voting against. Similarly, among right-wing conservatives, there is general agreement across the language divide on financial reforms. The rich and tax-friendly areas commonly vote for them and the rural areas against.

Over the last twenty years differences in the views of German and French Swiss voters on social policy, business, and world issues have grown more pronounced. The left-right division has coalesced around the language groups, helped by the growth of the media giants and the decline of small regional newspapers. There has been an erosion of traditional religious boundaries within the language regions, and an increase in individual campaigns. Whether this is a long-term trend is not yet clear. Certainly the Swiss regions are turning toward the ideas of their neighboring countries, which changes the national political landscape.

## WORK ETHIC

It should come as no surprise that such efficient and scrupulous people work long and hard hours, but it might not be widely known that Switzerland has not always been a wealthy nation and did not become one until the latter half of the twentieth century. The historic emigration of those seeking a better life proves this. Mainly in the rural and Catholic areas, working hard has been a necessary way of survival, and this ethic remains strong today. In the Protestant regions, the moral conviction that hard work leads to redemption has been the driving force.

The Swiss work an average of forty-two hours per week. Officially, full-time employees are entitled to vacation of only four weeks per year, less than in many other European countries (although many companies offer more, especially to older employees). Public holidays vary from canton to canton, but there are generally eight or nine. In 1985, in a referendum, the Swiss rejected a general increase in vacation entitlement from four to five weeks, and in 2002 they voted against the introduction of the thirty-six-hour week. Strikes are rare and workplace absenteeism is low.

Apart from long hours, work entails a high degree of honesty and integrity that ensures follow-through as well as punctuality, and people do not bring their personal lives into the office. Working overtime is not uncommon and is even expected, mostly in the German-speaking regions. In Latin-speaking Switzerland there seems to be more of an adherence to regular working hours and greater accommodation of home and family life. The German Swiss consider the French Swiss to be less reliable—starting work later, enjoying longer working lunches, and not replying to e-mails within the day.

Being well-organized and keeping your work space tidy is important. The Swiss also pay careful attention to personal care and grooming. They are quite materialistic, and quality is important. The expensive watch under the well-pressed sleeve may be expected but is never flaunted. The Swiss have little regard for anything ostentatious. They work hard for their money and equally hard at saving it. Not risk takers by nature, living on credit has not been the preferred way of doing things in the past, but there are signs that this, too, is gradually changing among young people today.

# chapter three

# CUSTOMS &
# TRADITIONS

## FESTIVALS AND CELEBRATIONS

Traditional customs are alive and well all over
Switzerland, with a rich variety not only from
region to region, but also from village to village.
Religious festivals, the farming year, and the
events of history, national and cantonal, are all
celebrated in one way or another. If Swiss daily
life is a bit too rigid for your liking, the following
energetic, magical, and occasionally eccentric
customs will show you a side to the Swiss
character you might never have suspected.

### *Fasnacht* or Carnival

Basel is considered the place to be for carnival.
The city's celebrations are the best known and the
most extravagant. They can begin in the small
hours of the morning (the *Morgesträich*) when all
the street lighting is turned off to make way for a
procession of large, decorative lanterns. The
people are awakened by masked and costumed
figures drumming, playing flutes, and marching.
The *Morgesträich* traditionally starts on the

Monday after Ash Wednesday, at precisely 4:00 a.m. Music, processions, and plenty of noise carry on for much of the day. Typically, many costumes worn at the carnival reflect current affairs and events. Cafés and restaurants provide a forum for the *Schnitzelbank* tradition, where participants stand and declaim satirical verses about topical affairs. In addition to the main carnival, the part of the city known as Klein Basel has its own festival in January, where the *Wilde Maa* (wild man), *Leu* (lion), and *Vogel Gryff* (half bird, half lion) dance through the streets, while four jesters, known as *Ueli*, collect money from the crowds to help the poor.

## Tschäggättä

In contrast to the colorful and playful costumes seen during the carnival season elsewhere in Switzerland, one valley—the Lötschental in canton Valais—upholds a tradition involving ferocious-looking wooden masks. An unwritten rule allows only unmarried men to practice the custom. They wander around their village wearing demonic masks, sheep- or goatskin tunics, and gloves smeared with soot, taking the occasional swipe at anyone they meet (particularly young women). The *Tschäggättä*, as they are called (meaning piebald), are undoubtedly masters of the village during this time. The tradition stems from the time the valley was cut off from the outside world in winter. The masks are an expression of anarchy and rebellion by a peasant society that was largely dominated by the Church.

### *Sechseläuten* (Zürich)

This festival, on the third Monday in April, goes back to medieval times, when one of the city's traditional craft guilds held a nighttime parade complete with musicians and horseback riders. The idea caught on. Other guilds followed suit, and in 1839 the first coordinated *Sechseläuten* parade of all the guilds took place. The name *Sechseläuten*, meaning "chiming six o'clock," goes back much further in history. It celebrates the arrival of spring and the lengthening daylight hours that allow people to work until 6:00 p.m.

The festivities open on the preceding Sunday with a parade of children, mostly dressed in historical costumes. This is followed the next day by the parade of the guilds, which culminates at six o'clock with the burning of a giant snowman, or *Böög*, which is stuffed with explosives. A fire is lit under the snowman and tradition has it that the quicker its head blows off, the better the summer will be.

## Harvest Festivals

The end of summer is marked in many alpine areas by bringing the cows down from their summer pastures in the mountains. In the more populated areas, fairs known as *Chilbis* are held every weekend toward the end of September. Fall is the season of harvest, which means not only giving thanks to God, but also taking produce to market and stocking up for winter. Harvest thanksgivings are held in numerous places throughout the country. Children's games and market stalls invade village streets where the locals sample the traditional sweets of *Magen Brot* (cookies) and *Apfel-Chüchli* (deep-fried apples), or gather together under tents for a cheesy dish of *raclette*, *bratwurst*, wine, and beer, or hot specialty coffees.

Particular areas have interesting traditions. Charmey, in the Gruyère region, holds hay-cart races during its festival. The festival in Stans, the chief town of canton Nidwalden, is called the *Aelperchilbi*. Wild men and women, the "*butzi*," dressed in skins and moss, chase the children and throw them sweets.

## REMEMBERING HISTORY

Few customs can be linked to particular historic events, but Geneva's best-known holiday, the

*Escalade*, celebrated in early December, commemorates the city's defeat of the Roman Catholic troops of the Duke of Savoy in 1602. Tradition has it that quick-witted Mère Royaume hurled a bowl of boiling soup on to the enemy soldiers as they attempted to scale the walls. Today's heroic Genevans repeat her feat by making chocolate tureens filled with marzipan vegetables. Another custom marking a historic event is Geneva's fast day, held on the Thursday after the first Sunday in September. Originally a day of prayer after the St. Bartholomew's Day massacre of fellow Protestants in France in 1572, it is now associated with eating plum tarts. People were supposed to abstain from meat on a day of penitence, and plums happened to be in season.

---

### PUBLIC HOLIDAYS

**January 1** New Year's Day

**January 2** St. Berchtold's Day

**March or April** Good Friday, Easter Monday

**May 1** May Day

**May** Fortieth day after Easter

**June** Whitsuntide—Whit Sunday and Monday. Ten days after Ascension

**August 1** Swiss National Day

**December 25** Christmas Day

**December 26** St. Stephen's Day, Boxing Day

## PUBLIC HOLIDAYS

As well as the national holidays, below, there are also cantonal holidays, especially religious ones.

### National Day

August 1 is to the Swiss what July 4 is to Americans, or July 14 to the French. Swiss National Day is just over a century old, and it was only in 1993 that the hardworking Swiss agreed they could all take the day off. But the event it commemorates, the Oath of Confederation taken by the three original cantons, took place seven hundred years before. It's a day for speeches by politicians at all levels. The president always makes a speech from the Rütli meadow, and federal councillors and heads of communes address meetings all over Switzerland.

### Christmas

Christmas in Switzerland is becoming more and more commercialized, with stores beginning their festive displays before the end of October. Holiday markets add traditional flair once December arrives, and shoppers can browse through the adorned narrow streets of villages and the "old towns" in city centers, sipping *glühwein* and eating *heissi maroni* (hot chestnuts), and buying special Christmas cakes. Children look forward to this time when they can dip their own candles, or

*Kerze*, made out of sweet-smelling beeswax. At home they hang their *Adventskalender* (Advent Calendar), with pictures or chocolate surprises behind the doors. The traditional German Christmas cake, *Stollen*, is equally popular in German Switzerland, as is the making of specialty cookies for the festive season. In Ticino *panetone* is very popular.

Celebration begins on December 6, widely known as *Samtichlaus Tag*, or the Feast of St. Nicholas, the patron saint of children. (In the French parts Père Noël comes on Christmas Day only.) They leave shoes outside their door on the Eve of St. Nicholas for him to fill with mandarin oranges, nuts, and cookies. Since it is not Santa who brings presents at Christmas but the *Christkind* (an angel), this day in early December is when children in kindergartens and playgroups find out if they've been naughty or good. Don't expect the jolly, fat Santa of North American tradition, but a slimmed down and more serious version. He arrives accompanied by his sidekick, *Schmutzli* (or "dirty guy"), who is dressed all in brown, his face darkened with soot. It used to be said that *Schmutzli* would beat naughty children with a switch and carry them off in a sack to be eaten in the woods. Beatings and kidnappings are no longer spoken of today; instead *Schmutzli* hands out oranges and nuts while his superior delivers a stern lecture or two about good behavior. Presents are traditionally opened on December 24. Families in the German areas enjoy meat fondue called "*chinoise*," and in the French areas they indulge in specialties such as *foie gras* or truffles, followed by special desserts of cakes and cookies. Christmas Day is a time for family to be together, visiting one another or enjoying the outdoors—sledding, walking, or skiing.

**New Year**

New Year's Eve (December 31) is also St. Sylvester's Day, when the last person in the household to rise from bed is woken up with shouts of "Sylvester!" The last child to arrive at school is also dubbed Sylvester. In the evening, bonfires are lit in the mountains and church bells are rung to alert all that the New Year is about to be ushered in.

***Dreikönigstag/ Trois Rois*** **("Three Kings' Day")**

Today's celebration of Epiphany or "Three Kings' Day" dates back only to 1952. On January 6 each year, people buy *Dreikönigskuchen/Galette des trois rois*, a plump ring of buns, one of which contains a small plastic king. Whoever ends up with royalty between their teeth gets a crown, and can tell everyone else in the family what to do for the rest of the day. *Dreikönigstag* was revived in this form by (you guessed it) the bakers, just over half a century ago. In the Christian calendar, Epiphany is the day after the twelve days of Christmas, when the three kings visited the stable where Christ was born. Traditionally it involved a lucky loaf that would protect the house from evil spirits. In pagan times, it was the end of the twelve *Rauchnächte*, dark and gloomy nights when spirits walked abroad. Today it is a public holiday in Catholic areas of Switzerland.

**Easter**

Easter is a time for specialty chocolate shops and bakeries to show their wares. People enjoy an extra long weekend, and children decorate eggs and take part in Easter-egg hunts. This is probably not very different from what the average foreigner is used to, but cultural variations abound if you take a closer look at individual cantons. In Mendrisio, in the southern Italian-speaking canton of Ticino, on the last Thursday of Lent, the locals stage a performance of the biblical passion play, complete with Roman soldiers and horseback trumpeters. This is followed on Good Friday with a more somber procession during which two sculptures, one of the dead Christ and the other of his mother, Mary, are carried through the streets. In Romont, in a French-speaking canton, Fribourg, in western Switzerland, "weeping women" carry scarlet cushions through the streets bearing the symbols of Christ's passion. The streets of the town echo with chants and prayers. In Nyon, near Geneva, the town's fountains are decorated with flowers, ribbons, and eggs, reflecting an old German tradition of celebrating the melting of the snows and the return of water to the fountains. In canton Valais, certain villages uphold the old Easter tradition of distributing bread, cheese, and wine. Luzern is the venue of the annual *Osterfestspiele* , or Easter concerts. On Easter Sunday, people passing through the village of Rumendingen, in canton Bern, might be surprised to see people throwing wooden clubs (*Knütteln*) around. This game originated because it was forbidden to indulge in traditional sports on Easter Sunday. The oldest player begins by throwing a club, and the others try to get their clubs as close as possible.

RELIGIOUS LANDSCAPE
During the Reformation Switzerland became a haven for Protestantism, and until the mid

twentieth century was a predominantly Protestant country—so much so that only a generation ago mixed marriages were problematic. The influx of immigrants from southern Europe in the 1970s has since changed the balance. Membership of all Christian Churches has shrunk in recent years. In a wide-ranging poll of Swiss attitudes taken in 2000, only 16 percent of Swiss people said religion was "very important" to them—far below their families, their jobs, sports, or culture. Another survey published in the same year showed that the number of regular churchgoers had dropped by 10 percent in ten years. Among Roman Catholics, 38.5 percent said they did not go to church, while among Protestants the figure was 50.7 percent. Only 71 percent of those asked said they believed in God. The demand for church baptisms, weddings, and funerals has fallen sharply in the last thirty years. The 2000 census showed that the Catholic and the mainstream Protestant Church (the Reformed-Evangelical) had lost in both absolute terms (the number of members) and in relative terms (their share of the total population). The small Jewish community had remained more or less unchanged. Recent immigration has brought members of other faiths to Switzerland, in particular Islam and Orthodox Christianity.

Even if the Churches are no longer relevant in many people's lives, both Roman Catholicism and Protestantism have played a key role in shaping modern Switzerland and the way in which Swiss people see themselves.

# chapter four

# MAKING FRIENDS

## DISTANCE AND SMALL TALK

Foreigners new to Switzerland often find themselves discouraged by how hard it is to get to know the Swiss. Often perceived as cold and reserved, they can initially seem an unwelcoming bunch. Keep in mind that this is only on the surface and making friends will just take time. There is a clear division between the private and the public realm in Swiss culture, and although understanding this will not necessarily help you to befriend a Swiss, it will certainly remove a potential obstacle.

The Swiss maintain close ties with those they grew up with in their home town or village, and those with whom they went to university. Breaking into this inner circle may take a while because the Swiss don't take friendship lightly. Sharing anything personal with someone they don't know well is simply not in their nature. The point at which they determine that they know you well enough to open up is difficult to gauge. Once a friendship is made, however, you'll have a friend for life. Friendship grows with time, as does a sense of trust.

To outsiders, who are used to a speedier route to having a chat, the distance the Swiss maintain is difficult to understand. They are generally wary of people who open up quickly. Quite frankly, they don't know how to handle it and take the view that people who do this tend to be superficial. American and British people are used to small talk as a way of engaging in conversation. Quite comfortable at cocktail parties, they may talk to several people in the course of an hour, sharing bits of their life and moving on. The Swiss, on the other hand, although quite capable of small talk, prefer to engage in lengthy discussion.

## GREETINGS

Hellos and good-byes in the German-speaking regions can be a bit of a mixed bag and at first confusing to foreigners. What's used with friends can often be different from that used with acquaintances or strangers. The most often heard greeting in the German part is the Swiss German "*Grüezi.*" If more than one person arrives together they will say "*Grüezi mitenand*" or the more informal "*Hoi z'sämme.*" A casual "*Hoi*" or even an accented English "*Hallo*" or French "*Salut*" can commonly be heard among friends. When saying good-bye, the Swiss German "*Uff wiederluege*" (this is the Basler version) is common, or else "*Ade,*" which is an abbreviated version of the French "*Adieu.*" Italian influence is strong in this respect and friends who know one another well will say "*Ciao*" or the Swiss German "*Tschüss.*" In the French regions, the standard "*Bonjour*" and "*Au revoir*" suffice. With friends, the French Swiss will greet someone with "*Salut*" and depart with "*Ciao.*"

Shaking hands is very common and is considered correct behavior in Switzerland. When arriving at a small party, it is customary to make the rounds, shaking each person's hand and introducing yourself to people who don't know you. When you leave you should again shake people's hands and say good-bye. If you haven't introduced yourself or been introduced, don't expect people to approach you and introduce themselves. They are respecting your boundaries and think that, when you are ready and willing, you will approach them. This can seem quite unfriendly to Americans and the British, who may expect the new person in the room to be made to feel at home. It's not that you aren't welcome, just that you're being given your space.

It is not uncommon even for children of kindergarten age to shake hands. Every day when they say good-bye, each child shakes the hand of his or her teacher. (In the French parts, small children give their teachers three kisses, rather than shake hands.) Even at this young age, if they are playing at a friend's house, when they say good-bye and leave with their mothers, they will shake hands with one another and with the mother of their friend. Often, if someone meets a friend with children, they will greet the children by shaking hands with them as well. It is also quite common to see teenagers shaking hands naturally when greeting and leaving each other.

## KISSING

Friends greet one another with three kisses on the cheeks. This is primarily between women and between a man and a woman, but in the Latin parts men sometimes kiss each other. In the

French parts, it is not uncommon for women to give kisses to the children of a friend, even when meeting them for the first time.

### Kissing Etiquette

Ariane was invited home by a new friend, not yet having met her husband or children. When she arrived, she kissed her friend and the children, but shook hands with the husband and the four other guests. When she left, she kissed all the adults (the children were in bed).

The point at which one graduates to kissing from hand shaking is not always clear cut, but to the Swiss this means you have moved into their realm of friendship. If a foreigner kisses an acquaintance at what may to the Swiss seem too early in the relationship, it may make them feel uncomfortable. Similarly, if a Swiss senses that a foreigner is not comfortable with kisses, he or she will shake hands in order not to embarrass. If you are married to a Swiss, or in a close relationship with one, expect your partner's friends to offer kisses quite soon after meeting you, perhaps even after a single dinner party, and you wouldn't be doing anything amiss by initiating this yourself in such a situation. However, people can know each other for years as acquaintances and never exchange kisses. It is one way of maintaining a distance that they feel comfortable with. There is another way, and that is through words.

## DOING "*DUDSIS*"

Unlike English, German and French have both a formal and an informal word for "you." In the German Swiss regions using the formal "*Sie*" instead of the informal "*du*" can be a way of keeping a relationship on less intimate terms, but it also shows respect. In the French areas where corporate structures are more hierarchical and status is more openly acknowledged, people tend to remain on formal terms much longer. One starts with "*Monsieur*" and "*Madame*." Later one might move to first names, but stick to the formal "*vous*" rather than the familiar "*tu*." This is a magic formula, showing that you trust somebody, while respecting the hierarchy or age difference.

As we have seen, the moment of moving from acquaintance to friend can be ambiguous, but it is aided by a ritual known in the German parts as "*dudsis*," which is an official agreement, so to speak, between people to greet each other less formally: namely, to use the informal "*du*" instead of "*Sie*" when speaking to one another. Traditionally, people would meet over lunch or

culture smart! **switzerland**

after work for a drink and toast one another to acknowledge the change of relationship. Today, this agreement does not have to be such an event, and can even be reached through an e-mail exchange. In the French part the drink ritual accompanying the passage from from *vous* to *tu* is called "*schmolitz.*" Friends drink wine together, holding their glasses with arms entangled while saying the other person's first name.

## THE EXPATRIATE COMMUNITY

For foreigners visiting Switzerland for a while, there is an extensive network of clubs, media, and commercial outlets for the international community, and it is quite usual for foreigners to use these means to socialize and meet friends. A lot can be said for such organizations and businesses. They make life easier for expatriates and can be particularly welcoming if you are an accompanying spouse or in some other position that makes it difficult to meet people. The workplace may prove frustrating, as there is a clear distinction between work and private life in the German regions. It is not customary for the German Swiss even to talk about their home life at work; colleagues are just that and not necessarily friends. In the Latin parts, however, socializing at work is more common, and sought after.

Today English is spoken on a regular daily basis at home, at work, or in school by more than a million of Switzerland's residents. According to the latest census of the federal office for statistics, 73,422 expatriates living in Switzerland claim English as their mother tongue. Like Switzerland itself, the English-speaking community is highly organized—there are more than 230 English-language clubs, schools, and other organizations. Twenty-one specifically American or Swiss American clubs have more than 10,000 members. In Geneva, for instance, the international community (the U.N., humanitarian organizations, and multinationals) is so important that the expatriate can easily live here for many years without really interacting with Swiss people.

## ATTITUDE TOWARD FOREIGNERS

If you are invited to someone's home or to a dinner party, you'll most likely find people welcoming the chance to use English, which is a trendy language in Switzerland. English words and phrases have been appropriated by the

German Swiss to add color and flair to their speech (less so among Francophones). They can also be seen in graffiti and publicity slogans around the country. English is hip, fashionable, and spreading. It is particularly handy for publicity, since otherwise four separate language versions would have to be produced. The Swiss are good at using brand names without meaning—"Sugus"(a candy), "Cennovis"(a yeast extract spread), and "Alinghi" (the name of the Americas Cup winner)—which all the linguistic communities can relate to.

The Swiss are used to interacting with foreigners, and will usually make allowances for any apparent neglect of certain formalities. However, there are things that simply go against their nature and make them uncomfortable. You will get much further by making an effort to understand their viewpoint.

The Swiss may be surprised by foreigners' frustrations. They see themselves as extremely helpful, particularly in work situations, and concerned for the well-being of newcomers. They would never leave them to fend for themselves but would take responsibility for settling them into a new position. Most Swiss, if introduced by a friend to a foreigner, feel accepting of this person. Quite often, however, they think that Americans and the British don't understand what it's like to have to communicate in another language, and don't appreciate the effort it takes to do this effectively.

### Mutual Misunderstanding

A Swiss woman, unsure of what her British colleague was saying, told her she didn't know what she meant. Complete understanding was very important to her and she wanted to clarify what she had heard. The English woman's response was to repeat herself in exactly the same words. This was not what her colleague had been hoping for. Used to communicating in various languages, the Swiss woman had wanted her to rephrase her sentence in words that were less complicated and easier to grasp. She was disappointed when they could not come to a better understanding.

## INVITATIONS HOME

Dinner parties are a reflection of the Swiss approach to friendship. They are an opportunity to spend quality time with one another. From birthday parties to summer barbecues, expect a lengthy sit-down meal. Make sure you are punctual and expect to take your time.

Changing seats to mingle with different people is not customary, and can be perceived as rude, or can suggest that you're not interested in the people you are with. Switching seats when coffee is served is acceptable, however. Before starting to eat, in German-speaking Switzerland say "*En guete,*" and in the French part, "*Bon appétit.*" With wine, always wait until the host or hostess says "Cheers" ("*Prost*" or "*Santé*"). When clinking glasses or simply raising them to one another, it is important to look each of the guests in the eye as you do so.

## THE *APÉRO*

Something you'll have to become acquainted with if you're going to get to know the Swiss is the *apéro*. The Swiss may hold a stand-up drinks party to bring a group of friends together, without the formalities of an organized dinner party. Normally only a couple of hours long, this might be a gathering after a cultural event, a farewell to a colleague at work, or a way of introducing yourselves in a new neighborhood. If the time for an *apéro* is given as 6:00 p.m., it is appropriate for you to drop in at any time after that, but you're not meant to stay late into the evening. On offer will be a selection of wines, mineral water, and orange juice, as well as neat

and efficient finger foods that won't complicate
matters when it is time for the prerequisite
shaking of hands.

## COFFEE CULTURE
Continental Europe's first Starbucks coffee house
opened in Zurich in March 2001. Switzerland was
picked as the chain's inaugural site because of its
coffee culture. Don't expect to see the Swiss lining
up with their to go cups and ordering a skinny
cappuccino before rushing off to the office. They
are much more likely to hang out in one of the
Italian-style coffee bars, which offer real Italian
coffee and all that implies: good discussion and
quality time with friends that could last for hours.
This is also a way for moms to meet up with one
another, along with their kids. Where the
Germans often include cakes in their coffee ritual,
the Swiss stick to the caffeine kick and stimulating
conversation.

## NEIGHBORLY BEHAVIOR
Swiss neighbors will, more than likely, wait for
you, the newcomer, to make initial contact. The
last thing in the world they would want
themselves is to have someone drop by
unannounced. It is not so much an untidy house

they are worried about as wanting to have a formal visit. They would prefer to be prepared with coffee and an ample amount of time when someone comes into their home. Any apparent lack of interest when you have just arrived is only to allow you enough space to get settled. It also reflects their own attitude of self-reliance, and although they can be extremely helpful if asked, it's unlikely they'll inquire whether you need help. It is not unheard of for neighbors to welcome you with a bottle of wine (on your doorstep), but it is more likely that they will maintain a respectful distance, not wanting to be too intrusive.

### *Getting to Know You*

An American woman, Anne White, was annoyed when she saw an elderly Swiss neighbor peeking at her mailbox. Immediately she jumped to the conclusion that here was an inquisitive person poking her nose into her business. It didn't help matters that this woman had not greeted her on the street the day before. The next morning, as the American was out shopping, the woman approached her, saying, "*Grüezi, Frau White, ich heisse Frau Bollag.*" The American took a moment to realize that her neighbor had learned her name from her mail in order to introduce herself properly.

Once you have moved in, it is a good idea to find a way to introduce yourself properly. This could be at a chance meeting in the hallway, or by organizing a more formal *apéro*. It should be mentioned, however, that *apéros* might not be appreciated in areas outside the cities, where people tend to keep to themselves until they know you better. That said, these same rural neighbors may consider you to be standoffish if you don't greet them with an agreeable "*Grüezi*" when you enter the local shop or restaurant, so an effort should be made not to seem unfriendly. In the cities, just a few miles away, you'd appear like Crocodile Dundee in New York if you made such an overture to passersby. Where virtual anonymity ends and congenial greetings begin is difficult to determine as rural communities are not necessarily remote. For example, just fifteen minutes outside Zürich, in some of the outlying villages, people are already beginning to adopt different attitudes toward greetings and honoring personal space.

## TAKE THE OPPORTUNITY

In the cities you may find more opportunities to mix with people in your community than in rural towns and villages. Sometimes, in younger areas, neighbors will organize *boules* (French bowls), or even table-tennis tournaments.

Mothers who regularly meet at the local playground find convenient avenues to friendship through small children, and organize coffee mornings either at a coffee shop or in their homes. If you are learning the language, this may be a good way to practice. If you ask a Swiss person if they speak English, they will, more often than not, say "Yes, a little," and then proceed to answer your questions in very competent English. You'll probably often hear, especially among mothers, "Why don't you speak German to me, and I'll speak English to you?" so that they can brush up on their own linguistic skills.

**Small Breakthroughs**

Once they feel they are on the same wavelength as you, the Swiss are able to laugh at themselves.

A Swiss woman and an American woman periodically met up at a playground near their homes. While their children played, the Swiss woman enjoyed practicing her English and prodded the American to speak in German so that she would learn the language. This soon became a habit, and the American grew comfortable asking her friend questions when she stumbled over unfamiliar words and phrases. One afternoon, the Swiss, who had brought along a thermos of hot coffee, asked the American if she would like some more. "I'm okay," the American replied. In response to a look of slight surprise, she followed it with, "Is there an equivalent in German to this type of reply, or do I have to say, "*Nein danke*?"

"No, we say just that, '*Nein danke.*'"

The American looked at her friend with a grin, "You don't care if I'm okay or not do you? You just want to know if I want some coffee!"

"Exactly!" replied the Swiss, and the two broke into an easy laugh.

# chapter five

# THE SWISS AT HOME

### *HEIMATORT*

The *heimatort*, or home town, is the cornerstone of Swiss society and is a good example of the deep roots that anchor people's loyalties. As we have seen, the Swiss citizen feels a strong sense of duty at a local level that overrides any nationalistic sentiment. Swiss people inherit their place of origin from their fathers and maintain a strong affiliation with it throughout their lives. It is their *heimatort* that you see written on a Swiss passport, not their actual place of birth, even if no one in the family has lived there for generations.

It is not uncommon to find people who have never moved away from their *heimatort*. The

Swiss prefer to stay where they grew up. They don't have to move away to attend university, and quite often will seek work close to home following graduation. Because of this, it is easier to understand the tightly-knit friendships that develop and are maintained over the years between people who have grown up together. Often, too, because they don't move away to further their education, many Swiss students remain at home throughout these years. If they have to move in order to attend a university, they're likely to return home on weekends, keeping the ties strong. It is important to point out, however, that the strong roots of the average Swiss in no way inhibit them from learning about the rest of the world. On the contrary, living in such a small country seems to encourage a desire to explore beyond their borders and take a strong interest in other people's cultures and languages.

## LIVING SPACE

Switzerland has a large number of one- and two-person households. Many older people live alone or in retirement homes, rather than with their children or their relatives, as they used to, though children are staying on in the same house with their parents for longer. Many couples live together for several years before getting married, or instead of marriage. It is considered important to finish one's education or to become financially established first. Families are generally small, with only one or two children, and generally live outside the big cities.

If at all possible, people aspire to buy their own home. Property is very expensive, however, and the level of ownership is the lowest in Europe at 30 percent. Things are changing, but it is still the norm for the Swiss to live in rented apartments. Such apartments are in high demand and supply is short, making rents quite steep. Housing can account for about 25 percent of your net income, or more in some areas.

Buildings vary from large apartment blocks to smaller two- or four-family dwellings. On the outskirts of cities and in the wealthier neighborhoods, you will see more houses. Many buildings are old but are well preserved and extremely well maintained. Frequent renovations are the norm, and even if a building looks a century or more old, the interior is likely to be modern and tasteful.

Unfurnished, however, means just that. Don't expect closets or light fixtures, as the departing tenants are legally obliged to take these with them. By law, all houses have to have a basement, which can be used as a shelter in time of war, and the storage place in the basement of a building helps to compensate for the lack of space in the apartment.

Apartments and houses are not necessarily small by international standards, but they date back to when things were done a little differently. Traditionally, Swiss people did their dairy shopping daily, most likely on foot, at the local shop. Refrigerators had to be large enough for just a single day's shopping. Although the corner store is disappearing, the small refrigerators haven't changed, and nor has the attitude of the Swiss, who seem quite unaccustomed to stocking up for a week at a time. This is beginning to change somewhat, as there are more women working, but not to the degree you would see in North America or Britain. Consequently, even if apartments are quite large and spacious, don't expect the kitchen (the "Barbie kitchen," as one foreigner referred to it) to be spacious or have large appliances.

## THE LAUNDRY ROOM

Space problems explain a lot in Switzerland, and the home is no exception. Very few apartments, even if quite large, have a big enough bathroom or kitchen to install a washing machine. Both dishwashers and washing machines have to be 55 centimeters wide, while in all other European countries they are 60 centimeters. Even if you had the space for one, the cost of having to produce machines just for Switzerland has made the price of a washing machine unaffordable for many.

The rules governing the use of the shared laundry room of an apartment building typify the Swiss need for order and mutual respect. These have been satirized (by the Swiss and foreigners alike) in books and magazines as a symbol of "Swissness." The laundry room is sacred ground. Individual time is booked, if you're one of the lucky ones, once every two weeks. (In some buildings, it's every three weeks.) This is your designated "laundry day," which drives even the most die-hard outdoors people inside on sparklingly clear spring days, to adhere to strict rules and washroom etiquette. Expect a slap on the wrist for all those in violation. Clothes have been known to be taken hostage, and held under lock and key, until the delinquent tenant who had the audacity to wash out of turn sheepishly shows up to claim the load. Getting all your laundry done in one day can be a complicated business when each wash cycle on the average machine takes two hours, and you can't run it during "quiet time." Not all apartments are so strict, however, and it is becoming more common for people to buy their own machines.

Perhaps with the complexities of daily life—shopping every day, challenges with laundry, and space issues—there is a feeling of inflexibility about the place. Interestingly, in conversation with the Swiss, you will often hear them referring to someone approvingly as "uncomplicated." This is undoubtedly an attribute that is a welcome reprieve from the rule-based society they live in.

### The Swiss and Drafts

Be prepared for an odd national quirk. No matter how hot and stuffy a room may become, never open a window, or even suggest opening the windows on opposite sides of a room. And certainly, if you have passengers, don't think of opening the windows of your car while driving. The reason? As is known by all Swiss from infancy, this would result in a draft or movement of air across the skin, which is commonly held to be the cause of all disease, and probably much of the evil in the world. You may encounter this attitude when traveling in a cramped bus or tram on a hot summer's day, when open windows are deliberately shut once the vehicle begins to move. If nothing else, it proves the Swiss love saunas!

## LIVING CONDITIONS

Most foreigners are taken aback by the rules and regulations of living in Switzerland, especially in apartments where people live in close proximity to one another. Many of the rules are related to space issues. There is normally a local by-law or house rule that you must not make noise during the lunchtime period between 12:00 and 2:00 p.m. and often also after 10:00 p.m. Very possibly the stereotype of the Swiss being too uptight would dissolve if it weren't for the protocol in most apartment buildings in Switzerland that disallows residents from running a nice hot relaxing bath after 10:00 p.m. After all, what hardworking Swiss or stressed-out mom can fit a bath in any sooner? But indeed, this applies in many apartments and you may have to live with it. Other examples of making too much noise are cutting the grass, hanging pictures, or playing music too loudly. If you're going to have a party, be sure to inform your neighbors.

Bags will become an important part of your daily life. Save paper shopping bags in order to use them the next time you buy groceries. No sensible Swiss would waste a perfectly adequate bag, nor would they pay thirty Rappen/centimes for a bag every time they shopped (which, as we already know, is often!). Fill your expensive community-issued garbage bags with unrecyclable material only, and never leave them outside your door in the way of neighbors before collection day. You are also expected to keep all areas that are shared, from the laundry room to the garage, neat and tidy, and never leave anything like bicycles (or even shoes) in the hallway, out of respect for the other tenants.

## EDUCATION

The education system in Switzerland is highly decentralized. The Confederation may regulate policy overall, but the financing and implementation is the responsibility of the cantons, which leave many practical matters to the municipal education authorities. The teaching material and subject matter can also vary from canton to canton. By North American standards, Swiss education tends to be both more conventional and strict, with less emphasis on individualism.

### Compulsory Education

Children can begin kindergarten as early as four years of age in some cantons, depending on their date of birth. Most children attend for two years, but this can be altered according to a child's age and development. Primary school starts at six or seven years of age and lasts until children are twelve years old. Secondary school, the last stage of compulsory education, lasts three to five years depending on the type of school and the canton. It is during this period that students are channeled into an appropriate educational or commercial program that will prepare them for a career or a university education.

**Vocational Training**

Four out of five people in Switzerland have completed at least the second stage of education, which lasts three years. Roughly 64 percent of those who continue into the second stage complete a vocational course (*Lehre* in German, *apprentissage* in French). The vast majority of such courses last three or four years, depending on the chosen field, and operate under the day-release system, where the trainee works for an approved company and attends a vocational school for one or two days per week. Students may choose from about three hundred recognized apprenticeship categories. The most popular fields are mechanics and engineering, office work, and sales. Young German-speaking people are more likely to choose this path than their French-speaking counterparts. Apprentices who pass the final exam at the end of their basic training are awarded a federal diploma that is recognized throughout the country. The proportion of young

Swiss choosing to take up apprenticeships is falling. It dropped from 65 percent in 2000 to 58 percent in 2002. On the one hand, more students are choosing to stay on at school, and on the other, more job seekers are looking for work that they can start full-time without further training.

## Universities

Pupils who wish to study at university must normally attend a secondary or high school for three or four years. They take the final exam — known in German as "*Matura*"—when they are eighteen or nineteen. After passing this test, they earn a graduation certificate that allows them to choose the university they would like to attend. An increasing number of young people are awarded this certificate. In 1990 the figure was 12 percent, in 1995 16 percent, in 1998 18 percent. The number of university students is low in comparison with neighboring countries because students of technical subjects receive their higher education at specialized institutes, which are equivalent to universities in many other countries. In 1998, 9 percent of twenty-seven-year-olds had a university degree, up from 5.9 percent in 1980, largely as a result of the increase in the number of women students. There are three universities in the French-speaking part of Switzerland (Geneva, Lausanne, Neuchâtel), and five in the German-speaking part (Basel, Bern, Zürich, Luzern, St. Gall). Fribourg University is bilingual German-French. Since 1996 there has been a university in Italian-speaking Ticino, with its main base in Lugano. There are Federal Institutes of Technology in Lausanne (*École Polytechnique Fédérale*, or EPF) and Zürich (*Eidgenössische Technische Hochschule*, or ETH).

**International Schools**
Switzerland has long had a reputation for exclusive, top-of-the-line, private education, and the international schools in the country are no exception. The price is high for an education that provides a more international approach but may be invaluable, especially to foreign students who are in the country for a short period of time and don't want to disrupt their studies. Many of the schools are accredited for various British and American diplomas and certificates, including the International General Certificate of Secondary Education and A-levels (British), the American College Test, the Scholastic Aptitude Test, the Test of English as a Foreign Language (American), and also the Swiss *Matura* examination.

**Pisa Study**
Education became a hot political topic in Switzerland following a 2001 study by the

Organization for Economic Cooperation and
Development (OECD) called the Pisa Study
(Program for International Student Assessment).
Switzerland was given one of the worst ratings in
the OECD, which triggered widespread debate
among educators about how to improve the
system. Teachers, experts, and bureaucrats are
working to revamp a system that they agree needs
to be more flexible in terms of tracking (those who
are university material and those who are not), and
that has a tendency to sort by social background.
Successful educational systems in other countries
have, in the past decade or so, undergone extensive
transformations in regard to streamlining at a
young age, and it is those that have changed from
the old tracking system that are now receiving a
higher grade on an international scale.

## MILITARY SERVICE

Historically, Switzerland's neutrality has been
based upon armed deterrence, and its 400,000-
strong citizen army is, theoretically, the largest in
Western Europe. It used to be the case that many
CEOs in large Swiss companies were also officers
in the army. An old-boy network cultivated in the
army is still evident in some of the most powerful
industries in the country. Today, success in
business is not necessarily equated with being a

high-ranking officer. Perhaps too many days away from the office were having an effect. Formerly, every able-bodied Swiss male had to serve a three-week refresher course every second year until the age of forty-two (fifty-two if a senior officer), following the initial fifteen-week training course taken at twenty years of age.

Today the armed forces are being redefined. Both the age and the time served are being reduced to twenty to thirty years of age and 260 days respectively, along with major cutbacks in the overall defense budget. Women can volunteer to serve in the armed forces and can now join all units, including combat units. There are already about 2,000 women in the army but, so far, they have not been allowed to use weapons for purposes other than self-defense.

Although the new armed forces, known as Army 21, will be smaller, they will still be based on the militia system, but with a much larger professional element. In a break with tradition, Swiss soldiers have recently participated in international peacekeeping operations, and this is likely to happen more in coming years.

## DAILY LIFE

The Swiss usually start the day with a breakfast of *Gipfeli* (croissant), bread, jam, and cheese with juice and coffee. Much of daily life is governed by long working hours, especially in the German parts. A two-hour lunch break is still common in the Latin regions.

Children rarely spend the whole day at school, and depending upon their age will attend school at different times. It is normal for children to have lunch at home, but in some districts there are after-school facilities—"*horts*" in German, "*cantines*" in French—where the children can have lunch and be supervised, if both parents are working. These are few and far between, and are not as convenient as in North America or the U.K. The school system is undergoing changes that will make hours more consistent across the age range.

Switzerland is an outdoor enthusiast's dream, and on weekends you'll find the Swiss out of doors, taking advantage of the country's many lakes, pools, and walking and cycling trails in the summer, or the many ski resorts and sledding hills in the winter.

## SHOPPING

Stocking up for the week is not part of the Swiss mentality. Grocery shopping, for the most part, is a daily ritual. The small grocer is still around but has largely been replaced by large supermarkets. Cities and towns all have outdoor markets on specific days where fresh vegetables, baked goods, flowers, and arts and craft items can be bought. On Saturdays, or specified weekdays in the cities, people go to the larger markets to sell used furniture amid the produce. Swiss consumers expect a very high standard in products and services and are willing to pay for it. They want top quality that is also good value for the money.

Generally, shops open at 9:00 a.m. and close at 6:30 p.m., Monday to Friday, and are open from 9:00 a.m. to 5:00 p.m. on Saturdays. Lunch breaks from noon to 2:00 p.m. are common in smaller shops. There are shops in service stations, train stations, and airports that may stay open until 9:00 or 10:00 p.m.

Many foreigners are surprised by the early closing hours. There have been many attempts to introduce longer opening times, but these have been overwhelmingly rejected on the grounds that unsocial working hours undermine family life. In areas close to the French border, some people go to France to shop, where shops stay open till 9:00 or 10:00 p.m., as well as on Sunday mornings. Online grocery shopping has also become increasingly popular.

There are two typical Swiss stores that are worth knowing about—Migros and Coop. Migros, which was founded on strong moral principles as a cooperative by Gottlieb Duttweiler, aims to bring the consumer closer to the producer. It sells inexpensive "homemade" copies of top-quality branded Swiss products, and its philosophy prohibits the selling of cigarettes and alcohol, unlike its direct competitor, the Coop.

## WORKING HOURS

Commercial offices are generally open between 8:00 and 9:00 a.m. and 5:00 and 6:00 p.m., Monday to Friday.

Government office opening hours vary. Some start at 7:15 a.m. while smaller ones start at 9:00 a.m. The offices are closed for lunch from 11:30 a.m. or noon to 1:30 or 2:00 p.m. Closing time is between 4:00 and 5:00 p.m.

## RESIDENCE PERMITS FOR FOREIGNERS

There are several types of residence permits. Among them are seasonal (type A), annual (type

B), and permanent (type C). Initially, most people are given a B-permit, which must be renewed annually. A B-permit restricts the holder to living in the canton that has issued the permit. It will also indicate the reason for being in Switzerland. It may say "*Verbleib bei Ehegatten*" for someone accompanying a spouse, or "*bei Eltern*" for children under eighteen accompanying their parents. If it lists the name of an employer, it is both a residence and a work permit. Depending on the country of origin, a B-permit holder is usually given a C-permit after five years of continuous residency. Holders of C-permits are permitted to change jobs and cities of residence in Switzerland without applying for a new work permit. The holder is also free to leave the country for up to two years without losing permanent-resident status. A C-permit also facilitates business and property ownership.

## VISAS

Most people who are not citizens of a Western European country will need a visa to enter Switzerland. Check with the Swiss embassy or consulate in your home country to be sure. If you need a visa for employment purposes, a letter offering employment must be taken, along with a passport, to the embassy or consulate in your country of residence. On receipt of the applicant's acceptance of a job, the Swiss employer applies to the Cantonal Aliens' Police for a residence permit. Once the application is approved, a visa will be granted.

E.U. nationals whose countries are members of the Schengen Agreement (which eliminates border controls within the Community) have preferential treatment in Switzerland, which has bilateral agreements with many member states.

# TIME OUT

It will come as no surprise that people with so little free time organize it well when they have it. The Swiss have been characterized as cool and reserved, which can make them sound an unsociable lot. However, once away from their busy week at work, what brings them the most satisfaction is coming together to share some quality time.

## CLUBS AND ASSOCIATIONS

The average Swiss German belongs to five clubs. These can be anything from informal groups like the *Stammtisch*, which is a beer-drinking or card-playing group of old friends, to more formal political, cultural, professional, or sports organizations. If you are planning to stay for a while, several clubs and organizations for English-speaking foreigners help the settling-in process and provide a good opportunity to

meet people. But if you are looking for the chance to integrate into the community, clubs and associations at the local level are an excellent way to do this. Courses are popular with the Swiss, and there are several organizations that offer a wide variety of adult education. At the largest, Migros Club School, over three hundred subjects are offered, the majority of them being language lessons (Swiss German is offered), arts, crafts, and sports.

For many Swiss men, social life includes membership of a guild. Historically, guilds were craft or trade associations. Today, they are similar to North American organizations like the Shriners. They can be social clubs for people who enjoy good food, drink, and conversation, or political clubs of like-minded and economically influential men. Membership of the guilds is by invitation only and is reserved for family members of current guild members and for those who have achieved a certain status in society.

In the Latin parts of Switzerland such formal associations are less widespread.

## RESTAURANTS

Wherever you are in Switzerland, you are never far from a restaurant, and a good one at that. There are approximately 27,000 in the country!

Whether you are walking the streets of a major city, skiing next to the Matterhorn, or taking a forest walk on a Saturday afternoon, you are sure to find a place for a delicious hot meal, or for sitting down while chatting over a steaming rum tea while you warm your bones. Whatever the Swiss are doing in their leisure time, restaurants and local tastes play a significant part in the overall experience. Prices in an average restaurant are slightly higher than in other Northern European countries, and if you are looking for something a little more elegant, prices can be very high indeed. Make a note of opening times, though. In many places at lunchtime you can't get anything to eat after 2:00 p.m.

Unlike its German neighbor, Switzerland does not have a strong pub culture. Drinking, particularly in the German areas, comes second to the fine dining and conversation so much valued by the Swiss. This by no means implies that the Swiss don't appreciate a choice glass of wine or shot of *grappa*; these just play a background role for people sharing a good meal.

Cuisine in restaurants of the various linguistic regions displays influences from neighboring countries. The Swiss Germans are known for succulent soups, and pork and veal dishes with cabbage and potatoes. *Rösti* is a shredded potato dish eaten at any time of day. Rich sauces and desserts add a final distinctive touch to their menus. *Bircher-müesli* (muesli with fruit and yogurt) is a favorite meal on its own, not as breakfast but for lunch, with a milky coffee called a *Schale*. Wine is grown throughout German-speaking Switzerland that can either, depending on its quality, be appreciated on its own or go into the fondue pot. The German Swiss especially don't always have time for a long sit-down lunch, and although fast-food chains are on the rise, the average Swiss in the German regions is content to grab a *bratwurst* or *cervelat* sausage from an outdoor grill with a crusty roll, if on the run.

## Fondue *and* Raclette

These traditional dishes, and the way they are eaten, provide a good example of how the Swiss like to socialize. In the Middle Ages, alpine herders discovered that if their local cheese was placed close to the glowing coals of the fire, the outer layer would melt and could be scraped off and enjoyed warm with their meal. This is how *raclette* (which means "scrape") originated. Since then, its preparation, like that of its melted counterpart, *fondue*, has evolved from a practical ready meal to something that is conducive to lengthy round-the-table discussion.

French Swiss cuisine is influenced by the fact that some of the largest lakes in Switzerland are in the French region. Here, lake fish are eaten, possibly even more frequently than cheese *fondue* and *raclette*. Most of Switzerland's wine is produced in the French regions, and wine, of course, plays an important part in French Swiss gastronomy, for both drinking and cooking. The French have always been wine drinkers, whereas the Germans have traditionally drunk beer. The drinking of wine among German-speakers is a recent fashion. In the French areas, beer is used as a summer thirst-quencher, especially with lemonade (known as a "*panache*"). Although they prefer a long lunch, the French Swiss may turn to a convenient *panini* stand on the street when running for an appointment.

Although the Italian-speaking Swiss would be quite offended if not regarded as thoroughly Swiss, their eating habits tend to be thoroughly Italian. Some delicacies, however, are particular to the people of Ticino, such as *torta di pane* (bread pudding with chocolate and raisins), and a sausage dish, *mortadella e lenticchie*. Risotto, noodles, gnocchi, and ravioli are representative of the truly Italian dishes that have made it to the Swiss table. If in a hurry, that good old standby pizza remains a popular choice.

Of course, restaurants of all the various regions can be found throughout the country, and Swiss from all backgrounds sample one another's dishes. Getting down to basics, however, if you had to summarize a few choice items common to all, they would be salad, cheese, good bread, and chocolate. When the restaurant-going Swiss tire of the expense of eating out, and resort to their cupboards at home, they're sure to have these items somewhere in their kitchens. Oh yes, and let's not forget the coffee.

## CAFÉ SOCIETY

It's not clear which the Swiss love more—coffee or the socializing that goes with it. The taste (and strength) of the coffee, generally the real Italian stuff, is key. So, too, is the atmosphere of the café in which they meet, often for hours at a time. Most cafés also sell spirits, which visitors will probably find very expensive. The legal age for drinking in Switzerland is sixteen.

Friends may get together in a busy, smoky café; families may choose one with ample space for the children. In both cases, the reason for being there is to share each other's company. Sometimes, in the German areas, you'll see friends playing the traditional card game "Jass" in restaurants, at the *Stammtisch*, or table reserved for regular customers. The Swiss would rather do this than sit at home watching television on weekends. They watch less television than any other Europeans, and they also read more newspapers.

> ### TIPPING
> Expect a 15 percent service charge to be included on most hotel, restaurant, and bar bills. This service charge is also included in taxi fares and in the price of having your hair done. For this reason, tip only if you've had extraordinarily good service. Flagrantly offering a large tip is considered ostentatious and not in good taste.

## RETAIL THERAPY
Zürich has the world-famous *Bahnhofstrasse*, home to the large department stores—where you can buy a great range of goods, including a Swiss

Army knife at a reasonable price—along with smaller designer boutiques and specialty stores. The equivalent, although less famous, shopping street in Geneva is la Rue du Rhône. Wealthy tourists who can afford the steep hotel prices generally continue their shopping spree here for designer clothes and luxury goods such as top-of-the-range Swiss watches. Everyone will want to buy specialty chocolate, such as Sprüngli's. Heimatwerk is an interesting store chain where one can buy handmade Swiss souvenirs. Stores may open at 8:00 or 9:00 a.m. and close at 6:30 or 6:45 p.m., Monday to Friday. On Saturday they open from 8:00 a.m. and close at 4:00 or 5:00 p.m. On Sunday stores and shops are closed. There are shops at main train stations in most cities that keep longer hours, staying open until 9:00 p.m.

## BANKING HOURS

Banks are normally open from 8:00 or 8:30 a.m. to 4:30 or 4:45 p.m., Monday to Friday. They are closed over the lunch hour only in the smaller villages. One day a week, most banks are open late, the day depending on the bank's location. Generally they are closed on Saturdays. You will find banks open on Saturday in large shopping centers and in tourist destinations, and banks at airports and change offices at railway stations are even open on Sundays. Automatic twenty-four-hour banking centers in major cities will allow you to exchange foreign currency into Swiss francs, purchase foreign currency, buy traveler's checks, give you change, and will even rent you a safety deposit box.

## ART, MUSIC, AND POPULAR CULTURE

Although Switzerland is not generally considered a great European cultural center, culture is an integral part of Swiss life. Despite the fact that many artists, particularly architects, have had to leave the country because of limited opportunities, the public's enthusiasm for high art and cultural events remains undiminished. The Swiss avidly attend ballets, take full advantage of their numerous museums, and eagerly anticipate the annual outdoor concerts that attract artists from around the globe and the international film festivals.

With over nine hundred museums, Switzerland has one of the densest museum networks in the world—one for every 7,500 people. The number has tripled since 1950 alone. A "Museum Pass" costs 90 sFr. a year and grants access to all Swiss museums. As visitors and locals alike frequent the larger museums, however, the smaller museums of local history are struggling and face financial difficulties. There has been an upsurge in the establishment of prestigious museums by private collectors, such as the Beyeler Foundation and the Museum Jean Tinguely in Basel and the planned Klee Museum in Bern.

Today Switzerland boasts the greatest number of artists in proportion to its population. Historically many artists of Swiss origin, such as the modernist painter Paul Klee, the sculptor Alberto Giacometti, the great architect Le Corbusier, and the filmmaker Jean-Luc Godard, made a name for themselves outside the country. Switzerland was considered too "provincial," and Swiss artists drew their inspiration from abroad.

During the First World War the art scene flourished in Switzerland because of its neutral status. The famous Cabaret Voltaire in Zürich's old town was the birthplace of Dadaism. It was here that the immigrant painters and poets who had sought refuge in the country created the Dada art and literary movement as a protest against the senseless violence of the war. The movement quickly inspired artists and writers in New York, Berlin, and Paris, and is regarded as the catalyst for the emergence of Surrealism.

During the Second World War, Switzerland was a refuge once again for artists of all disciplines.

Influenced by Constructivist ideas and the ideals of the Bauhaus, the Swiss artists Max Bill and Richard Paul Lohse founded the movement of geometrically-based painting and sculpture called Concrete Art. The Zürich concrete school was an important influence in twentieth-century art internationally. Today the Foundation for Constructivist and Concrete Art is a museum in Zürich dedicated entirely to its works.

### The Art Lovers

About thirty years ago, a Picasso exhibition was held in Basel. The city thought it would be nice to buy one of the paintings shown, but the people of Basel had to vote on it. They overwhelmingly accepted this costly idea by more than 70 percent. Picasso was so touched by the reaction of Basel's citizens to his art that he offered the city a gift of two additional paintings.

Theater, in all national languages, opera, and ballet thrive in Switzerland. One English-speaking company is doing particularly well. In 1954, a group of English-speaking people came together to create a drama club because of a lack of English-language entertainment. Today, they not only perform regularly to sold-out audiences, but have been honored by their adoptive country. In 2002, the Zürich Comedy Club (ZCC) was awarded the Max Geilinger Prize, which has been presented only twelve times since 1969 to

individuals for their promotion of the English language in Switzerland. For the first time, with the ZCC, it was awarded to an organization. Max Geilinger (1884–1948) was a Swiss author. His wife was English and they were both passionate about all things English. Presenters praised the club saying, "The Zürich Comedy Club doesn't play in the background of our society, but rather plays an important role on the cultural landscape. During its forty-eight-year history, the ZCC has secured a firm place in the cultural life of the city of Zürich and has stamped its influence on the development of the literary and cultural connections between Switzerland and the Anglo-Saxon world in a refreshing way."

Switzerland has a lively music scene with an abundance of pop, rock, and jazz open-air festivals throughout the summer. One of the best-known is the Montreux Jazz Festival, which brings in stars from all over the world. The Easter concerts at the Lucerne Culture and Convention Center, the Menuhin Festival in Gstaad, and the

Snow Symphony in St. Moritz are
highlights for classical music lovers.
For information on all concerts,
www.ticketcorner.ch is a useful Web site.

## OUTDOOR PURSUITS

Outdoor pursuits are central to Swiss leisure time.
The country itself is a playground for young
and old. Where else can you see middle-
aged women sledding down a hill?
There are more than 31,070 miles
(50,000 kilometers) of
designated footpaths in the
country, and walking is a
national pastime in both summer and
winter. *Waldhütte*, or forest huts, can be rented in
summer or winter, and are ideal for parties. You
can build a log fire to keep warm and there's no
need to worry about disturbing the neighbors.

The Swiss take full advantage of their beautiful
Alps, and it's difficult to spot a poor skier
anywhere on the slopes. They expect their World
Cup skiers to do them proud, and are highly
critical if they fail to beat the (currently)
dominant Austrians.

In summer, the *Autobahn* is dotted with cyclists
of all ages. Swimming pools, lakes, and water
parks are essential to any family from June to

September. With its many lakes, Switzerland has a very strong sailing tradition. There have been jokes that the country could no longer be thought of as a "*Skination*" anymore since it had become a "*Segelnation*" ("sailing nation").

In addition to sailing, the Swiss enjoy rowing, ice hockey, gymnastics, soccer, golf, riding, shooting, paragliding, and adventure sports like canyoning, rock climbing, and mountaineering. In general, "wellness" is extremely popular with the Swiss, and there are several world-class spa resorts they can choose from.

# chapter seven

# TRAVELING

## WHERE TO STAY

The Alps have always been a formidable obstacle
to traveling, not only to, but within, Switzerland.
Before the early nineteenth century, the poverty of
the countryside and its difficult and
dangerous terrain made rather
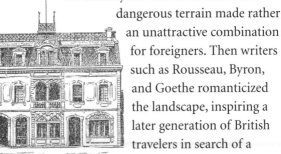
an unattractive combination
for foreigners. Then writers
such as Rousseau, Byron,
and Goethe romanticized
the landscape, inspiring a
later generation of British
travelers in search of a
challenge. A lucrative tourist
trade developed. Legendary hoteliers such as
César Ritz built some of the best hotels in the
world, ensuring Switzerland's standing as a
competitive tourist destination. Today
Switzerland is still known for its fine hotels and
for its world-class hotel management schools.

No matter where you travel in the country, you
are unlikely to come across a bad hotel. If the style

of the Grand Old Swiss Hotel is too much for
your tastes or your pocketbook, you will be more
than comfortable in a quaint family-run bed and
breakfast. Vacation apartments, usually rented for
a week at a time, can provide reasonable family
vacations. You can find what suits you best, from a
single- to a five-star rating, but book early for the
high season. The Swiss are becoming avid
campers and caravanners, and it is quite easy to
find a site in a breathtakingly beautiful valley, or
next to a serene lake. Some eighty youth hostels in
the country provide budget accommodation, but
to use them you must be a member of either the
Swiss Youth Hostel Federation (SYHF) or the
International Youth Hostel Federation. Family
membership is also available.

## SKI RESORTS

The glorious setting of the Swiss Alps has, for over
a century, drawn tourists in search of outdoor
adventure. Today, they come for more than the
long pistes and mountain air. Switzerland's
vibrant resort villages are famous for their
elegance and cosmopolitan flair.

Ski resorts offer plenty of accommodation of
different kinds, from vacation apartments and
chalets to expensive hotels. Some major ski resorts
are listed in the appendix on page 160.

## DRIVING

Roads in Switzerland are efficiently marked by a color-coded system. Green signs indicate freeways. Blue signs mark regular roads. White signs are for smaller roads, and yellow signs show paths for walking or roads closed to vehicle traffic.

If you are driving in Switzerland, you will need an annual freeway permit, or *vignette.* This will cost you about forty Swiss francs, but if you get caught without one, you'll be fined a hundred Swiss francs on the spot. Of course, you can forgo the freeway permit and take a more circuitous route through the countryside. It may take you longer, but you will see some devastatingly beautiful scenery along the way.

If you own a car, you will be subject to an official serviceability control test — *Motorfahrzeugkontrolle* (MFK), *contrôl des véhicules (à moteur/expertise)*—every three years. New cars need to pass the test every five years, even if there is a change of ownership. Owners are contacted by a test center when it is time to bring their car in.

Apart from this official upkeep, the Swiss take good care of their cars, keeping them clean and in good condition. By law, motorists have to have a red emergency triangle stored inside their car within reach of the driver's seat in case of an accident or breakdown. Rather annoying for foreigners is the legal requirement to change from summer to winter tires in winter; not to mention the winter equipment, such as tire chains, needed in certain areas.

The minimum age for a driver is eighteen years. The legal blood alcohol level is 50 milligrams of alcohol per 100 milliliters of blood—soon to be further tightened—and if you are caught driving above the limit, the penalty is stiff. If convicted, you will lose your license for at least a year, receive a large fine of at least 1,000 Swiss francs (this amount increases according to the size of your salary), and you could even be imprisoned. Fines for speeding are set in accordance with how much above the limit you were traveling. The country is punctuated with automatic radar-triggered roadside cameras. Traffic lights are also rigged with these machines, and if you run a light, you'll be fined 250 Swiss francs.

Holders of a foreign or international driving license can drive in Switzerland for up to a year before having to apply for a Swiss license. When applying for one, you can obtain an application form from your canton's motor registration office, or from an approved optician. If you choose the latter, you can get the requisite eye test at the same time. Once you have your Swiss

license, it is valid for life. Members of Swiss
motoring organizations such as the Automobile
Club of Switzerland or the Touring Club of
Switzerland can call the service number 140 (a
twenty-four-hour service) for free help.
Nonmembers can also call, but the service will
be expensive.

## TRAINS

It is not essential to have a car in Switzerland. You
can get pretty well wherever you want hassle free
on the network of 3,900 miles (6,300 kilometers)
of transportation lines that include trains,
trams, trolleybuses, and cableways.
Two thousand kilometers of these
are private, operated by some
hundred private railways or
cantonal governments. Public
transportation is a viable option
for the Swiss themselves, the
number of users being double the
average of other major European countries.

Efficiency and order being the hallmark of
Switzerland, you can bet your train will arrive on
time. Early morning commuters will start to
exchange worried glances should it be a couple of
minutes late. Normally maintenance work or bad
weather is all that stands in the way of a train

being punctual. The entire transportation network of buses, trains, and boats is so well synchronized that making connections is never a problem. The Swiss federal railways are referred to by their initials and according to the regional language—SBB (*Schweizerische Bundesbahnen*) in German, CFF (*Chemins de Fer Fédéraux*) in French, and FFS (*Ferrovie Federali Svizzere*) in Italian. Although they complain about the expense, this method of transportation is used by the Swiss more than by any other Europeans. It is well worth inquiring about the plethora of discounted fares and season tickets. Bicycles can be rented from most railway stations and can be taken on the train, but you must pay extra. More recently car-sharing has become fashionable. This inexpensive form of car rental involves traveling by train to your destination, having booked a car which will be waiting for you when you get there. (See www.mobility.ch.)

## HEALTH

Another service that puts Switzerland at the top of the list for quality and efficiency is its health-care system. It has the highest ratio of doctors to patients in the world. Health insurance premiums run second only to North America and Sweden, but in Switzerland you won't have to worry about waiting lists or quality of care. The Swiss would top another list if it weren't for the Japanese, who have the longest life expectancy. In Switzerland the life expectancy for women is eighty-one, and for men it is seventy-four. Challenging this stellar statistic is another one that is not so impressive. The number of smokers in the country is the third highest in the world.

Everyone living in Switzerland has to have health insurance. Once you've received the bill from your doctor, you pay it and then notify your health fund or insurance company, which will reimburse you for up to 90 percent of it.

"Wellness" is an epidemic in Switzerland, and the Swiss indulge in an assortment of therapies in their world-famous spas to combat the aging process. Alternative medicine is not as peripheral here as in North America or Britain, and is even covered by Swiss health insurance. Walk into a pharmacy—*Apotheke* in German, *pharmacie* in French—and the pharmacist is just as likely to suggest a homeopathic or herbal treatment for your ailment as something more mainstream. Many pharmacies in the cities are open late into the evening, and several even provide twenty-four-hour service. If a pharmacy is closed, the details of the closest "emergency pharmacy," open 24/7, will be posted in the window.

Switzerland's crime rate, in relation to other Western countries, is low. By any measure, this is a safe country to live and travel in. There has been an increase in the last few years of incidents of petty crime and pick-pocketing. The numbers are small by comparison, but this is something you should be aware of in large public areas like train stations.

# chapter eight

# BUSINESS BRIEFING

## THE SWISS ECONOMY

The IMD (International Institute for Management Development), one of the world's leading business schools, located in Lausanne, releases an annual report called *The World Competitiveness Yearbook*. This is a comprehensive survey of international competitiveness that uses the criteria of economic performance, government efficiency, business efficiency, and infrastructure to analyze the way a nation's environment sustains its competitive position. It features sixty national and regional economies, which are divided into two groups: those with populations of more than 20 million and those with less than 20 million. Switzerland, in the latter category, slipped in 2003 from third to fifth place in its group, falling behind Finland, Singapore, Denmark, and Hong Kong.

This verdict revealed a strong need for reform. Although it ranked high for having a well-educated work force, zero rate of consumer inflation, and an excellent social and economic infrastructure, Switzerland lagged behind when it came to innovation. It ranked among the lowest with regard to the government's ability to react quickly to economic changes, and low for the flexibility and adaptability of its population. It also ranked low for the openness of the national culture to foreign ideas. The slide in performance has been linked to difficulties confronting the country's finance industry, where, for the first time, the Swiss have taken the lead in reducing operational costs and staff, thus deepening the consequences of economic slowdown.

## LABOR RELATIONS

Switzerland is famous for its lasting "labor peace." By carefully balancing the various social and economic forces the Swiss have managed to avoid major social confrontations. There is a long-standing agreement by which employers and employees settle their grievances by negotiation, and strikes are rare. Trade unions, professional associations, and other pressure groups all have their say in the formulation of economic policies.

Freedom of association is protected by both the law and the constitution. Trade unions have the right to strike, though this is seldom exercised.

National and sectorial collective agreements are widespread, and there is union cooperation at the industry level in setting labor policy.

Most firms are relatively small—only 2 percent have more than fifty people on the payroll. The rules relating to collective bargaining vary across sectors and regions. Most negotiations take place at the company level. The law provides for official conciliation and arbitration of collective disputes at both the federal and cantonal levels, and if this fails, issues can be resolved through binding arbitration.

Employers are represented by the ZSAO (Central Association of Swiss Employer Organizations), which develops and implements overall policy for its members. The most important of these is the ASM (Association of Swiss Engineering Employers), which has about 600 member companies. Generally, the equitable distribution of profits encourages the continuing dialogue between employers and employees.

Working hours are generally from 7:30 a.m. to 5:30 p.m., Monday to Friday. Legally the working week is forty hours, but certain specific sectors operate a forty-one- or forty-two-hour week. Many offices operate flextime; this requires that all employees be present between certain hours, called "block time," and make up the required extra time by starting earlier, working later, or reducing their lunch hour. Working overtime is quite common in Switzerland. Most companies give four weeks' annual holiday, increasing to five weeks at the age of fifty, or for top management.

## PRESENTATION AND LISTENING STYLES

In their dealings, the German Swiss often seem overly critical by North American or British standards, simply because it is not in their nature to soften constructive criticism with praise. To them, they are just doing their job, and they see no reason to add personal touches to points that concern the business at hand. They don't display much emotion, either positive or negative, in business interaction. Even speaking too loudly can be interpreted as being overemotional. The Swiss will always try to avoid confrontation. They are wary of effusive behavior and mistrust it in others. This reserve can be a bit off-putting to foreigners when making presentations, because it is difficult to read their reactions. Your best course of action is to be well prepared, with all the facts at your fingertips, and then to get straight down to business. The French Swiss, on the other hand, have a much more discursive approach.

To foreigners used to a competitive environment, where selling oneself is crucial to getting ahead, Swiss colleagues can seem rather unenthusiastic. They see little reason for self-promotion when their work, quite clearly to them, speaks for itself. The German Swiss don't play the power game. They are not conditioned to stand out in any way and will avoid doing so. Even with top management, it is not always easy to identify the boss, or *chef,* from the rest of the staff. He most likely won't have a secretary, like his colleagues, and his office may not seem all that different from theirs. In French Swiss companies, however, you can usually tell who is boss—the French are more hierarchical and will relate deferentially to the *chef.*

Apart from a reluctance to exploit his status, there is another reason why a boss may not have more visible perks than the rest of his staff. Swiss business culture expects even top management to take care of things, such as arranging their own meetings, themselves. This is possibly an extension of the culture's high regard for personal responsibility, and may also account for the Swiss having to work such long hours!

The Latins of Switzerland generally value their private life more highly than the German Swiss, and are inclined to go home earlier. Given the choice, they would rather stay in for an *apéro* than for an urgent file.

## ETIQUETTE AND PROTOCOL

The Swiss, who are quite used to doing business with foreigners, are very accommodating and make allowances for them over certain breaches in formality (for example, addressing people by their first name upon meeting). However, when working in their country, it is imperative that the foreigner learns to understand their ways, so as to avoid the obstacles that can stand in the way of a productive business relationship.

A grasp of Swiss business protocol and etiquette can help make that all-important first impression, and facilitate future dealings. The American or English businessperson with a relatively casual approach to business dealings, and at ease in his own language, can be intimidating or even offensive, depending upon both the people and the circumstances.

The Swiss disapprove of tardiness. It is important that you show up on time for business meetings. Be well prepared, make your intentions clear, and come armed with all the relevant information. First impressions matter, so don't begin with casual small talk or by cracking jokes (especially in the German region). This will appear unprofessional and inappropriate.

Business dress is casual but conservative, and anything too ostentatious is frowned upon. You won't see many German Swiss colleagues wearing ties, unless they have a meeting with the chief executive. The French Swiss are more formal in this regard—depending upon the sector, you may be surrounded by ties. Whatever you wear, make sure it is clean and pressed. Neat and tidy is what it's all about. Open-plan office space is becoming more common, and keeping your desk in order is important and a reflection of good discipline.

Business meetings are formal. It becomes apparent here who is in charge, because senior management speaks first. Lower-ranking colleagues should not speak until addressed. Lower management always refer to the *chef* with the formal "*Sie*," and will do so until requested otherwise. Lower-ranking colleagues in the German regions often use "*du*," even soon after meeting. In the French regions, the formal "*vous*" is used with senior management and colleagues alike, and may not change after years of working together.

In the German regions, meetings are kept short and to the point. Anything other than business is not discussed, and even this is kept clear and concise. Clarity, or *Klartext*, is vital for effective business communication. Say what you mean, and ask for what you want—there is no time or reason for circumlocution. Equally important is follow-through. The Swiss take this very seriously. If you say you are going to do something, they will expect you to do it.

Getting straight to the point, however, does not mean ignoring good manners. On the contrary, the Swiss are very polite and courteous. When arriving at a meeting it is customary to shake hands with everyone present, and the same goes for when you depart. Address people by name (if you have forgotten, ask them). The handshake should be firm, and look the person straight in the eye in order to convey confidence and honesty.

It is customary to greet all your colleagues when arriving at work every day, and to acknowledge people in passing, even if you haven't been introduced. When you go for lunch, colleagues may say "*En guete*" or "*Bon appétit*," basically wishing you a nice meal. When leaving work in the evening, people often wish one another a pleasant evening.

Titles are not normally used when people introduce themselves (in order not to sound pretentious), but they will be by others in formal introductions. When arriving at a business event where people are milling about, introduce yourself before you start talking to someone, and avoid interrupting people unless you really have to. This applies during conversation, as well.

In the French areas the style is more relaxed. Although the Swiss French are more formal and hierarchical, they are also more group- and relationship-oriented, and more spontaneous. It is customary to take business acquaintances out for lunch, and here conversation can deviate from work matters into more general areas. As with the German Swiss, however, it is inappropriate to ask personal questions. Allow people to offer such information when, and if, they feel ready. Asking personal questions is considered too probing and is generally not welcomed, except from a close friend.

Avoid criticizing the country. Although the Swiss are not overly patriotic and may criticize their own country, it is not your place to do so. Try to avoid name-dropping—they won't be impressed. Avoid being ostentatious. The Swiss are not impressed by a show of wealth, and flaunting it will get you nowhere.

It is appropriate to exchange gifts after the culmination of successful negotiations. Do not give anything too large or expensive, as this will be considered vulgar. Suggestions include wine, chocolate (Swiss), and cigars.

## NEGOTIATING STYLE

The Swiss are anything but pushy, yet they have a way of getting what they want. This has a lot to do with the high quality of the goods and services they offer. There is simply no need for a hard sell.

The confidence this breeds allows them to take their time in any negotiations, and to consider carefully the points you make.

The Swiss are not risk takers. When negotiating a deal they require substantial information and persuasive argument from the parties involved before they will agree to anything. They will not respond to high-pressure tactics and will not rush into any decisions. They'll make you believe that you get what you pay for—you'll get quality if you pay the price. Keep in mind that the Swiss mean what they say and say what they mean. They are straightforward in negotiations and make a genuine effort to see all perspectives. They may even make helpful suggestions when it's not in their own immediate interest. Socializing happens only after the contract is signed. A contract is binding and it is important to adhere to it.

## TEAMWORK

The group dynamics among Swiss people working on a project differ significantly from those operating in American and British teams. Detailed planning is imperative in the initial stages with the Swiss, and tasks are clearly defined. It is at this point that team members contribute their expertise, and decisions made at this time are definitive. The Swiss are used to working independently after this, secure in their understanding of the brief and of what must be accomplished in a particular time frame. They may resent constant interruptions by their Anglo-American colleagues or bosses, and think that they are not being trusted to perform their tasks.

Americans, on the other hand, rely more on one another throughout the project for a constant exchange of ideas and for keeping abreast of developments. For them, analysis at the beginning is only meant to identify a broad outline of intermediate targets, leaving room for adjustment along the way. A Swiss trying to work within this team dynamic can feel frustrated or even embarrassed by constantly having to ask for information, thinking that he missed out on something in earlier meetings.

The initial planning phase characteristic of the Swiss can seem long and tedious to foreigners, who may be used to getting on with the business at hand, and dealing with problems as they arise. The Swiss, however, don't like leaving things to chance and won't appreciate the seemingly "trial and error" approach of American and British colleagues.

## DECISION MAKING

Swiss decision making reflects both their history and their present political system. Consensus is the rule of the day. The Swiss are capable of looking at issues from several different points of view, while maneuvering into a decision agreeable to all involved. Of course, this calls for a great deal of compromise (something at which they are very adept), and a considerable amount of time. The process is not so much a debate as a brainstorming session, until a decision is made. Whether this is actually to everyone's liking is not always apparent, as the Swiss tend to avoid taking a controversial stance in order to minimize conflict. Often the workable solution means that colleagues have, in their own individual way, thrown their weight behind the boss. A quiet resolution can therefore be arrived at, unbeknownst to a foreigner used to a more top-down style of decision making.

## PROMISE AND FULFILLMENT

The German Swiss are typically very reliable, and once they say they will do something, you can expect them to follow through with it. Their commitment will be the result of careful, time-consuming planning. They like to get all the facts, often from everyone involved, weigh them, and then make a final decision. Integrity in their dealings is yet another aspect that keeps the "well-oiled machine" running so smoothly. To a foreigner, this process can seem inflexible, because once a decision is made the Swiss expect it to be carried out. The foreigner should be careful with his choice of words, trying not to exaggerate or be overly optimistic with plans, because his Swiss counterpart will, more than likely, take his words literally. The Swiss can often seem cautious and slow to North American or British people, who tend to make decisions more quickly and on a provisional basis. Their decisions are often made informally, as they go along, and to the Swiss this can give the impression of being careless and unreliable.

## MANAGEMENT STYLE

The big companies that keep Switzerland running so smoothly have to be efficient in their own right. Their productiveness, like the nation itself, lies in a decentralized business structure, in which employees take pride and responsibility for the work they do. Also like the country, there is a strong emphasis on generally accepted rules and regulations instead of dependency on strong central authority. This corporate structure predominates because it is the *modus operandi* of the larger German-speaking region.

Swiss managers are cosmopolitan and normally have extensive international business experience. This is a natural consequence of Switzerland's export-driven economy. This international exposure requires Swiss management personnel to be well educated, multilingual, and familiar with foreign markets.

However, management styles do differ according to region in Switzerland. Those doing business with the French and Italian Swiss soon realize that management is more hierarchical and patriarchal. In the French regions, it takes a much longer time, if it happens at all, for colleagues to address one another in the informal "*tu*." The German Swiss are more task-oriented and egalitarian. Their managers have a cooperative leadership style that calls for active participation by the staff. They follow the rules more than the French Swiss, who turn more to a strong central authority for guidance. The role of the boss is central, but not dictatorial.

## DIFFERENCES BETWEEN GERMANS AND SWISS

Generally, Germans are more confrontational than their Swiss neighbors. The Germans, too, appreciate clarity in conversation, but tend to be even more direct than the Swiss, who have, by virtue of their more complex national makeup, learned to be more diplomatic in their relations with people. For those who speak both High German and Swiss German, there is a common feeling that High German is generally less friendly.

The Germans, unlike the Swiss, who from childhood have been taught to refer to an outside authority for guidance, tend to question rules and recommendations, and to judge things for themselves.

## WOMEN IN THE WORKPLACE

When it comes to women and work, Switzerland is a bit behind the times. National enfranchisement came as recently as 1971 (in canton Appenzell, full voting rights for women were not granted until 1991). An equal rights amendment was introduced in the constitution in 1981, the patriarchal marriage law was amended in 1985, and the barriers to a woman owning and running a business have now been lifted. Apart from general old-fashioned attitudes to women and work, male bonding, reinforced by military service, has put women at a distinct disadvantage when it comes to climbing the corporate ladder. There are comparatively few women in senior managerial or executive positions by North American or European standards, and women must work harder for less money and prove themselves.

More women than ever are choosing to stay on at work after having children, despite a general lack of childcare provision. The general perception is that salaries in Switzerland are high enough for a man to to support a family. Women who work rely mostly on a network of family and friends or an *au pair* to help care for their children. This is gradually changing, as facilities that provide children with lunch and after-school care are increasing, but this is not widespread by any means. Few mothers are able to hold high-level positions because they either cannot or choose not to work full-time.

Eight weeks' leave after birth is mandatory, but this does not guarantee continuation of pay. Most employers, however, will offer eight weeks' paid maternity leave. The Swiss people voted against entitling women to fourteen weeks' paid maternity leave in a 1999 referendum, although this is coming up for a new vote in 2004.

# chapter nine

# COMMUNICATING

**FACE-TO-FACE**

**Language**

For a country governed by so many rules and the need for order, Swiss German is a bit of an oddity. The Alemannic dialect known as *Schweizerdeutsch, Schwyzerdütsch, Schwiizerdütsch*, or *Schwyzertütsch* changes from area to area. Within the regional variations, however, there is consistency, and the different forms are mutually understandable. Even though it is a dialect of High German, the pronunciation of Swiss German is closer to Low German or Dutch.

Dialects in Europe are often associated with certain social or educational backgrounds. Not so with Swiss German, which is the everyday spoken language of all Swiss Germans. There are places that are exceptions, such as schools, parliament, and television news, where High German, otherwise known as "written German" (*Schriftdeutsch*), is used. German-speaking foreigners also use High German. Although Swiss

German is considered a spoken language, you may find Swiss authors and newspapers using dialect terms. It is difficult now to find a teenager in Switzerland without a mobile phone (or "handy") text messaging or e-mailing a friend. You can bet that in informal communication like this written forms of Swiss dialect are being used.

Most meetings with foreigners will be conducted in English. It is important for business people and travelers alike to appreciate the difficulties of speaking in a foreign language, even if your Swiss colleagues or business associates appear to be quite fluent. What they are capable of conveying is not always consistent with what they truly think or feel about something. Likewise, how they interpret your words, as well as your actions, may be far from what you expect. For the Swiss, especially, this is cause for concern, as being clear in intent is very important to them.

Knowing the languages of the Latin regions will help you in your business dealings there. Of course, knowledge of the language in the German regions helps too, but since Swiss German is a dialect rather than a written language, it is quite difficult to learn, and almost all foreigners learn the written High German. Swiss Germans are not always comfortable conversing in High German—

many positively dislike speaking it at all, especially to Germans—and when they realize you are English-speaking they will most likely start speaking to you in English.

**Humor**

It is an American and British custom to break the ice with humor, but with people they don't know, the Swiss would rarely think of initiating conversation in this fashion. Consequently, when it happens to them they may not know how to respond. In some cases, they may even feel that they are being made fun of. To add to their difficulties, humor doesn't always translate, and sometimes the Swiss simply don't understand the joke. This does not mean that the Swiss don't enjoy a good laugh, and they are not beyond self-deprecating humor when given the chance

The Swiss are in fact quite witty, and their humor can be subtle. Little will endear you to them more than your responding to their perceptive wit. Once touched by Swiss humor, you've reached an initiation point. It's a stage the passage of time brings about and one you should be on the lookout for. The Swiss appreciate it when someone is on the same wavelength, as they are not partial to having to explain themselves. If you can demonstrate this through an appreciation of their humor, great strides can be made toward friendship.

## Communication Styles

To the Swiss, being respected is more important than being liked, and their style of communication reflects this. In conversation, they may seem to be cold and distant to foreigners, unlike Americans, for example, who might come across as being too personal. The difference actually lies more in each party's interpretation of politeness.

Personal involvement for the Swiss is something that increases over time. It is a matter of trust, but also of what is appropriate. When communicating in public, they tend to respect one another's boundaries rather than cross them in search of further personal knowledge. This is not from lack of interest but from not wanting to appear too intrusive. Don't expect the Swiss to ask personal questions until you know them well.

We have seen that the Swiss place a high value on being direct and to the point, which can make them sound abrupt. If this should happen to you, there is one key point about their style of communication that you should bear in mind. Above all else, the Swiss wish to avoid confrontation. How then do they achieve this without the aid of those little social niceties the Americans and British are so conditioned to using, and which would sound downright patronizing to the average Swiss?

As in Swiss politics and business life, compromise and consensus are the key to successful social relations. Not surprisingly their basic communication style reflects this as well. The Swiss don't necessarily expect others to agree with them, and in the same vein they respect the other's point of view. They will listen intently, but in turn will present a well-thought-out case for consideration.

This is not to say that all conversations are deep and intense. It is a common misconception that the Swiss aren't capable of small talk. Most Swiss are inclined to exchange banter on a superficial level, as long as it does not touch upon particularly personal topics. It is fair to say this hasn't always been the case, however, and is a characteristic of a changing society. Today, articles in the Swiss business press—and the new profession of communications trainers—aim to convince Swiss managers of the value of small talk in paving the way to deeper relations.

Americans, on the other hand, have a greater desire to feel included, and to find something in common with those they are speaking to. Being polite means making attempts to relate to others through shared experience, and expressing interest in them. They are more dependent upon feedback from the person they are speaking to than the Swiss. Consequently, their conversation "dances" a little more, unpredictably, directed by the personalities involved. Generally speaking, Americans want to be liked more than respected, and maneuver toward one another rather than respect independence of thought. Americans might make definitive statements about one another as a way of showing interest or understanding. This simply wouldn't happen with the Swiss, who would never assume to know something about you.

Silence is interpreted in different ways as well. A British person, for example, may feel uncomfortable with long pauses in conversation and may perceive the discussion to be breaking down. By a Swiss, silence may be regarded as a sign of reflection, and they might make a point of utilizing it as a show of respect. On the other hand, it could also mean that they do not necessarily agree with what you are saying but don't want to offend, so they choose to be silent. In either case, it is honoring your opinion and should not cause anxiety.

This can all seem a bit complicated, and not knowing where to begin a conversation can leave foreigners quite tongue-tied. A few tips: don't criticize Switzerland; don't ask questions about the military; and don't crack a joke to break the ice. Express an interest in the broader issues of the day—world events or the latest referendum.

Expect the Swiss to be well informed. Generally they will have a clear opinion on most topics of the day. Possibly this comes from the political backdrop of a direct democracy, where people have to stay abreast of the issues of the day in order to vote responsibly in the many referendums that are held each year. The Swiss are very interested in other cultures, and would enjoy learning about your country. Even the weather, trivial as it sounds, is a light topic common to all that will avoid making anyone uncomfortable and can ease you into further topics of conversation. Often when the Swiss explain something to you, they will judge your reaction by your expression. Some gesture of approval will help facilitate deeper conversation.

Efficiency is paramount in Swiss business, and the best way to achieve this is by being very direct when making requests and giving instructions. Where a British executive, for example, might be able to give an indirect order (out of politeness) and achieve the desired result, such an approach would leave Swiss colleagues confused about both its urgency and its intent. Likewise, a foreigner in Switzerland might be offended by the abruptness of communication in the workplace. It is advisable not to take this personally. Your Swiss colleagues will almost certainly not have meant you to do so.

## TELEVISION, RADIO, AND ELECTRONIC MEDIA

SRG SSR idée suisse, known in English as the Swiss Broadcasting Corporation, is the largest provider of electronic media in Switzerland. Its services encompass seven television channels and eighteen radio stations, complemented by Web sites and teletext. SRG SSR media offer news, narrative, and background reports on politics, culture, society, and sports. Entertainment is also an important part of the schedule, with feature films, sitcoms, radio plays, shows, and discussion programs. SRG SSR services are broadcast nationally, but programming is made primarily for the country's separate language regions: German-speaking *Deutschschweiz*, French-speaking *Suisse Romande*, Italian-speaking *Svizzera italiana*, and Romansch-speaking *Svizra rumantscha*. The services offered by Swissinfo/Swiss Radio International are aimed at both a domestic and an international audience and are offered in nine different languages including English.

## NEWSPAPERS AND MAGAZINES

The most respected newspaper in the German area is the *Tages-Anzeiger*. In the French region it is *Le Temps. Bilanz*, and its French version *Bilan*, is a popular business monthly magazine. In the Romandie there is the magazine *Hebdo* (for *Hebdomadaire*, or weekly), which promotes the sense of "Romandieness." There is a monthly national English journal called *Swiss News*, which aims to inform the  English-speaking community about Swiss affairs, and the English-language magazines *Cream* in Zürich and *GEM* in Geneva.

## SERVICES
### Internet/E-mail
A higher percentage of the Swiss population own PCs than in the U.K., Germany, France, or the U.S.A. About 60 percent either own their own PC or have other online access. Whether in a major city, a rural village, or high in an Alpine ski resort, you are sure to find Internet facilities.

### Telephone
Switzerland has one of the highest numbers of telephones per capita in the world (over 600 telephones per 1,000 inhabitants). The telephone system is run by Swisscom, which controls the

network, but there are alternative companies you can sign up with that may offer competitive rates.

Most public telephones in Switzerland require phone cards, which can be bought at the post office or newsstands (kiosks).

---

### DIALING CODES FOR MAJOR TOWNS

**Basel** (0) 61

**Bern** (0) 31

**Lausanne** (0) 21

**Luzern** (0) 41

**Geneva** (0) 22

**St. Gallen** (0) 71

**Zürich** (0) 1 (Gradually being replaced by the prefixes 043 and 044.)

---

When using the phone, greetings and names are important. When answering the phone, the German Swiss state their family name first, in order to be identified correctly. When making a call, before saying anything it is customary to state your own name, whether you know the person you are calling or not. Some may do this even when calling directory inquiries, as it is a way of treating the operator with respect.

Let's say you're calling the doctor's office to make an appointment. The receptionist might answer the telephone with: "Dr. Schmidt's office. This is Frau Weber." Of course, this will be in Swiss German. It is quite acceptable to ask Frau Weber if she speaks English, but before you do so it is important to state your own name. This is common practice before the conversation begins. She will then greet you by your name, and will probably tell you that she speaks English "a little bit." Don't worry, that little bit is usually quite fluent. You can then proceed with your call in English.

In the French parts, you'd simply pick up the receiver and say "*Allô*," and in the Italian parts "*Pronto*."

The international dialing code for Switzerland is 00 41.

---

**SOME USEFUL TELEPHONE NUMBERS**

**Directory Inquiries:** 111

**International Assistance:** 1159

**Police and Emergency:** 117

**Fire Department:** 118

**Ambulance and Medical Team:** 144

**International Operator:** 1141

**Tourist Information:** (0) 1 288 11 11

## Post

The postal system is extremely efficient and reliable. Business hours are usually from 7:30 a.m. to 12 noon and from 1:30 or 1:45 to 6:00 p.m. on Mondays to Fridays, and from 7:30 to 11:00 a.m. on Saturdays. The hours may be restricted in smaller towns and villages. Main post offices in the major cities don't close for lunch and provide extra service (from 6:30 to 7:30 a.m., and then from 6:30 until between 8:30 and 11:00 p.m., Monday to Saturday) for urgent business outside normal business hours. These services are also available on Sundays from around 11:00 a.m. to 10:30 p.m. Some smaller towns offer this service, and the hours are usually listed outside the post office.

Most post offices stock envelopes and parcel packaging. You can also buy phone cards, garbage stickers, and road tax stickers here, and you can pay bills via the post office giro service. Larger outlets may sell office supplies, cards, and small toys.

Within Switzerland you do not need to use the CH code or the country name. It is important not to leave a blank line between the road and the place-name, though, otherwise the address won't be read by the selecting machine. The sender's address should appear either on the upper left-hand corner of the envelope or on the back.

Envelopes from abroad should be
addressed as follows:
Herr
Thomas Schneider
Stationsstrasse 29
CH-8306 Brüttisellen
Switzerland

## CONCLUSION

The best way of getting to know a country and its
people is to be open to experience, and then to
piece together our impressions. These often force
us to draw comparisons with our own way of life,
and can shed new light on our own assumptions
as well as the culture of our hosts.

Mark Twain once remarked, tongue firmly in
cheek, that, "Switzerland is simply a large, lumpy,
solid rock with a thick skin of grass stretched over
it." Those lumps, of course, include some of the
most magnificent mountains in the world, and
the social infrastructure that has evolved in this
Alpine meadow in the middle of Europe is
unsurpassed.

Mark Twain actually saw that beyond the scenic
beauty and orderly society there lies a more
profound Switzerland, which is not so easily

dismissed. "The struggle here throughout the centuries has not been in the interest of any private family, or any church, but in the interest of the whole body of the nation, and for shelter and protection of all forms of belief. This fact is colossal."

# Appendix 1: Ski Resorts

**St. Moritz**, in the southeastern canton of Graubünden, is among the giants of Swiss resorts. The name itself is so well-known that it is registered as a trademark and internationally copyright protected. Situated at 6,079 feet (1,853 meters) above sea level, in the middle of the Upper Engadine valley, the "dry, sparkling, champagne climate" of St. Moritz has become legendary, and the sun is reputed to shine, on average, 322 days a year.

**Davos**, also in Graubünden, is as well-known for its annual gathering of world and business leaders at the World Economic Forum as it is for its skiing. This resort is large and sprawling, and offers a variety of slopes for all levels of skiers. One of the most challenging is a 6,560-foot (2,000-meter)vertical drop that runs for nine miles (14.5 km) from Weissfluhgipfel to Küblis.

**Klosters** lies in the Prättigau valley, near Davos. It is named after a thirteenth-century cloister founded on the site. Smaller and less urban than Davos, it is a favorite of the British royal family as well as of German aristocrats.

**Gstaad** is the resort of the jet set. Situated in the Bernese Oberland, the slopes there are less challenging, but it's not only the skiing they've come for. This is the place to be seen, and if snow conditions are lacking, the shopping will make up for it.

**Mürren** sits picturesquely on a rock ledge overlooking the Lauterbrunnen valley in the Bernese Oberland. It's the closest resort to the slopes of the Schilthorn, which offer year-round skiing at 10,000 feet above sea level. Downhill and slalom skiing were developed here in the 1920s, and it is considered the birthplace of modern alpine skiing.

**Wengen**, in the middle of the Bernese Oberland, shares its extensive ski slopes with nearby Scheidegg and Grindelwald, the latter being the setting for the famous north face of the Eiger. Wengen, which is car free, is well-known for hosting a world cup downhill each year, the longest on the circuit.

**Interlaken**, at the hub of the Oberland's mountain railway network, offers astonishing views of the mighty Jungfrau *massif*. It is packed with American, Japanese, and lately also Indian tourists since it became one of Bollywood's favorite film locations.

**Zermatt**, Switzerland's most famous mountain resort, offers the longest winter ski season in the Alps. It nestles on a high plateau at the base of the mighty Matterhorn in the German-speaking part of the canton of Valais, in southwest Switzerland. The skiing on the numerous surrounding slopes is excellent, and the town has gained quite a reputation for its après-ski life.

**Arosa**, southeast of Chur in Graubünden, offers a refreshing change from the glitz and glamour of other resorts. It is a small, family-oriented ski area with extensive intermediate runs.

**Verbier**, near Martigny in the Valais Romand, is the jewel of French-speaking Switzerland. A stylish resort, it offers an abundance of expert runs and serious fun.

**Crans-Montana**, above Sierre, is situated on a sunny plateau facing south over the Rhône valley, with amazing views of the Matterhorn and Mont-Blanc.

**Les Portes-du-Soleil.** This huge area straddles France and Switzerland. It has 14 resorts, 209 lifts, 288 marked slopes, 151 miles (243 km) of cross-country skiing, and 9 snowparks.

**Les Diablerets** is a small resort in the Alpes Vaudoises, offering glacier skiing and the Botta 3,000 Restaurant (designed by Mario Botta). Situated at an altitude of 9,843 feet (3,000 meters), it has a unique panorama, and provides both a gastronomic restaurant and a self-service cafeteria.

# Appendix 2: Some Famous Swiss People

The current Swiss banknote series features prominent Swiss personalities. They are:

**10 sFr. Le Corbusier (Charles Edouard Jeanneret), 1887–1965**
Architect born in La Chaux-de-Fonds. His buildings and writings had a revolutionary effect on the international development of modern architecture.

**20 sFr. Arthur Honegger, 1892–1955**
One of the most versatile classical composers of his generation. Identified with the ultramodern school of music in Paris.

**50 sFr. Sophie Taeuber-Arp, 1889–1943**
Painter, sculptress, and craftswoman. With her husband, Jean Arp, she drew up the Dada Manifesto in 1918. One of the most talented of the Constructivist artists and influential in many different fields.

**100 sFr. Alberto Giacometti, 1901–66**
Sculptor and painter; born in Stampa. In Paris he joined the Surrealists, creating symbolic abstract constructions, before evolving his characteristic style of thin, rigid, tremulous figures.

**200 sFr. Charles Ferdinand Ramuz, 1878–1947**
Prolific writer from the French-speaking canton of Vaud, acclaimed for his pure prose style and descriptive power. Regarded in his lifetime as a regional writer, he is now recognized as a modernist who renewed the formal structure of the novel.

**1000 sFr. Jacob Burckhardt, 1818–97**
Historian of art and culture. Professor of History at Basel University 1858–93, he is known for his works on the Italian Renaissance and Greek civilization.

Other famous Swiss include the following:

**Jean-Jacques Rousseau, 1712–78**
Philosopher and writer, born in Geneva into a Protestant family of French refugees.

**Jacques Necker, 1732–1804**
Financier and statesman, born in Geneva. Reformed French

finances under Louis XVI. His dismissal was the immediate cause of the storming of the Bastille. Father of Madame de Staël.

### Johann Heinrich Pestalozzi, 1746–1827
Educational reformer, born in Zürich. His theories laid the foundation of modern elementary education.

### Marie Grosholtz Tussaud, 1760–1850
Modeler in wax. She learned her art from her uncle, J. C. Curtius, proprietor of wax museums in Paris from 1762. Tussaud was imprisoned during the Reign of Terror, and the heads of many famous people were brought to her for modeling. In 1802 she inherited her uncle's museums and moved to London, where she established Madame Tussaud's Exhibition, which continues to this day.

### Gottfried Keller 1819–90
Novelist, poet, and short story writer.
Best known for his book, *Der grüne Heinrich* (*Green Henry*).

### Johanna Spyri, 1827–1901
Author of the children's book *Heidi*.

### Henri Dunant, 1828–1910
Philanthropist and founder of the International Red Cross, born in Geneva.

### Ferdinand Hodler, 1853–1918
Painter and lithographer.

### Rainer Maria Rilke, 1875–1926
Lyric poet and novelist. One of the most influential writers of the twentieth century. Born in Prague, he came to Switzerland in 1919 and became a Swiss citizen.

### Carl Gustav Jung, 1875–1961
Psychiatrist, founder of analytical psychology. He held professorships at Zürich and Basel. He is seen by many as the founder of a new humanism.

### Paul Klee, 1879–1940
Modernist painter, graphic artist, and art theorist, born near Bern. Cofounder of the German abstract school Der Blaue Reiter and of the Blue Four movement.

**Gottlieb Duttweiler, 1888–1962**
Founder of the Migros cooperative.

**Jean Piaget, 1896–1980**
Psychologist and pioneer in the study of child intelligence.

**Max Frisch, 1911–91**
Novelist and playwright. After 1955 recognized as one of Europe's major literary voices. In the novels *Stiller* (tr. *I'm Not Stiller*), *Homo Faber*, and *Mein Name sei Gantenbein* (tr. *A Wilderness of Mirrors*), he was concerned with the search for personal identity. His best-known plays are *Biedermann und die Brandstifter* (tr. *The Firebugs*), and *Andorra*, a study of mass psychology.

**Friedrich Dürrenmatt, 1921–1990**
Prominent postwar playwright and essayist, who is often linked to the theater of the absurd.

**Elisabeth Kübler Ross, 1926–**
American psychiatrist born in Switzerland. After studying medicine at the University of Zürich, she became a pioneer in the field of thanatology, the study of death and dying.

**Ruth Dreifuss, 1940–**
Became Switzerland's first female president in January 1999.

**Martina Hingis, 1980–**
Tennis player. Born in Czechoslovakia and came to Switzerland as a child. Became the youngest-ever world number-one tennis player in 1997 at the age of sixteen.

# Further Reading

Bilton, Paul. *The Xenophobe's Guide To The Swiss*. West Sussex: Ravette Publishing, 1995.

Dicks, Dianne (editor) *Ticking Along With the Swiss*. Basel: Bergli Books, 2nd edition 1998.

Dicks, Dianne (editor). *Ticking Along Too*. Basel: Bergli Books, 1996.

Dicks, Dianne (editor). *Ticking Along Free*. Basel: Bergli Books, 2000.

Eu-Wong, Shirley. *Culture Shock! Switzerland: A Guide to Customs and Etiquette*. Portland, Oregon: Graphic Arts Center Publishing Company, 1996/London: Kuperard, 1999.

Hampshire, David. *Living and Working in Switzerland*. London: Survival Books, 9th edition 2004.

Honan, Mark. *Lonely Planet: Switzerland*. Hawthorn, Australia: Lonely Planet Publicatons, 1997.

Oertig-Davidson, Margaret. *Beyond Chocolate: Understanding Swiss Culture*. Basel: Bergli Books, 2002.

Singer, Heidi & Ingeborg Lasting. *Ultimate German: Basic – Intermediate*. New York: Living Language, 2000.

Steinberg, Jonathan. *Why Switzerland?* Cambridge: Cambridge University Press, 1996.

Studer, Peter and Walter Däpp, Bernhard Giger, Peter Krebs. *Berne—A Portrait*. Basel: Bergli Books, 2nd edition 1996.

Style, Sue. A *Taste Of Switzerland*. Basel: Bergli Books, 1996.

Teller, Matthew. *The Rough Guide to Switzerland*. London: Rough Guides, 2003.

Tuttle, Susan. *Inside Outlandish*. Basel: Bergli Books, 1997.

# Index

culture smart! **switzerland**

## Acknowledgment

Very special thanks to Ariane Curdy. As an intercultural specialist and
home-grown Swiss, she has provided invaluable professional and personal
insight into her intriguing country.